ALEXANDER OVECHKIN

Geoffrey Lansdell

OVER
TIME
BOOKS

The Publisher: OverTime Books is an imprint of Éditions de la Montagne Verte
Website: www.overtimebooks.com

Library and Archives Canada Cataloguing in Publication

Lansdell, Geoffrey, 1977–
    Alexander Ovechkin / Geoffrey Lansdell.

Includes bibliographical references.
ISBN 978-1-897277-40-9

    1. Ovechkin, Alexander, 1985–. 2. Hockey players—Biography. I. Title.

GV848.5.O95L36 2009   796.962092   C2009-903910-9

Project Director: J. Alexander Poulton
Project Editor: Kathy van Denderen
Cover Image: Courtesy of © Robcorbett I Dreamstime.com

We acknowledge the financial support of the Government of Canada through the Book Publishing Industry Development Program for our publishing activities.

 Canadian Patrimoine
Heritage canadien

PC: 1

Contents

Introduction 6

CHAPTER 1
The Ovechkin Family 18

CHAPTER 2
The Prodigy 30

CHAPTER 3
Ovechkin the Conqueror 45

CHAPTER 4
The Soviet Invasion 85

CHAPTER 5
The Russian Generation 106

CHAPTER 6
The Highlight Reel 128

CHAPTER 7
Broadcasting Alexander the GR8 137

CHAPTER 8
Quotes, Statistics, Awards and Records 164

Notes on Sources 181

Dedication

This book is dedicated to brotherly love. It therefore goes out to my twin brother, Sean; my older brother, Dayne; and to Alexander Ovechkin's two older brothers, Mikhail Ovechkin and the late Sergei Ovechkin.

Acknowledgments

I would like to thank my friend Dmitri Vitaliev for his interest in this project and for his insight into Russian history. I would also like to recognize that the tone and voice of this book is the product of listening to and incorporating the style and sound of a few brilliant broadcasters. These include Howie Meeker, Jim Robson, Tom Larscheid, John Shorthouse, Bob Cole, Harry Neale, Ron MacLean and Don Cherry.

Introduction

Alexander Mikhaylovich Ovechkin
Александр Михайлович Овечкин

Alexander Ovechkin has stepped into the limelight and made the planet pay attention. He is a scoring machine that runs on genetic strength and Russian perseverance. Built like a tank, Ovechkin brings a remarkably diverse arsenal of skills to the table. He has a lethal wrist shot that rises like a laser beam and rarely misses its target; he is an explosive skater who is blessed with blazing breakaway speed and tremendous lateral mobility; he never takes a shift off; he celebrates his goals like a kid in a candy store; and he is perhaps the first player in NHL history who regularly goes *through* would-be defenders by throwing *offensive* body checks. In other words, "He's Pavel Bure in Mark Messier's body," said Washington Capitals general manager

George McPhee, who drafted Ovechkin first overall in the 2004 NHL Entry Draft.

Alexander Mikhaylovich Ovechkin was born in Moscow on September 17, 1985, to Mikhail Ovechkin and Tatiana Ovechkina. The youngest of three sons, Alexander—or "Sasha" as his parents call him—grew up during a transitionary and turbulent period in Russian history. Born during the final days of the Soviet Union, Ovechkin is part of the first generation of Russians to have grown up after the Soviet Union's final collapse in 1991.

The timing of Ovechkin's birth is significant for a variety of reasons, but let's focus on his vibrant personality. On the ice, he is full of life. He loves to score, and unlike most stars, he works like a soldier. Off the ice, he has a compelling personality because he is sincere, direct and often poignant. When interviewed, he rarely relies on banal sports clichés. Instead, he gives you something to think about. When asked if his shot is his biggest weapon, he replied with this one-liner: "My biggest weapon isn't my shot, it's me." And then there is the ongoing feud with Don Cherry, which has made for some great television.

In March 2009, Ovechkin hit the 50-goal plateau for the third time in his four-year career, and he had prepared a little routine to celebrate the occasion. He scored the goal against Tampa Bay, and it came on a typical Ovechkin rush. Like Mike Gartner in the days of old, the right-shooting Ovechkin came down the right wing and used his quick release to fire a wicked wrist shot high on the goalie's glove side. As Ovechkin skated behind the Tampa net, he threw on the brakes, dropped his stick to the ice and held his hands over the stick as if it were on fire and too hot to pick up.

The routine was most definitely staged, and the goal came against the bottom-feeding Lightning, but so what? Ovechkin is a 23-year-old kid who loves playing hockey. Why should the public concern itself with the line between showmanship and showboating? According to Don Cherry and many other hockey traditionalists, the problem was that Ovechkin crossed a moral line. "You don't act like this goof," Cherry said. "This is goofy stuff. And the same guys that think this is entertainment, last year thought Avery was entertainment. You know what, it's the same church, different pew. It's the same junk, and don't you Canadian kids act like it."

When asked about Cherry's criticism, Ovechkin addressed the issue in his own unique way by staging yet another clever routine.

"Different minds," Ovechkin began with a nonchalant shrug. "Old people—they don't like when people show some energy, some emotions. So they're like robots."

This expressive and casual quality is what helps fans relate to Ovechkin, and it is also what distinguishes Ovechkin from some of the earlier generations of Russians who were often accused of looking indifferent and uninterested when playing the game. But along with players like Evgeni Malkin, Pavel Datsyuk and Ilya Kovalchuk, Ovechkin's generation is different because they never really experienced the effects of communism on their personalities.

When the first wave of Soviets came to the NHL in 1989, most of the players we saw had played for the Red Army teams of the 1980s that were coached militarily by Viktor Tikhonov. By contrast, today's Russian players never had to live in barracks away from their families. They were never told when to eat, what to wear and how long to train. They never had to censor themselves and subsume their personalities for the sake of the motherland. In other words, unlike the first wave of Soviet legends, this new generation of Russian players is not afraid to express themselves. When Ovechkin scores, he goes buck wild. When he loses, he swears and looks angry. When he wins, he is blissfully ecstatic. He plays and behaves like a man who is his own master.

The second reason for drawing our attention to Ovechkin's 1985 birth year is that he was born at a time of fundamental social change in the way the Soviet Union was relating to the West. By the time the '87 Canada Cup happened, the Soviet Union was on its last legs. With the liberal-minded Mikhail Gorbachev in power and beginning to draw back the Iron Curtain, there was less censorship of information, and it became easier to express oneself freely and to travel abroad.

In the hockey realm, because the Canada Cup tournaments were played on Canadian soil, Russian players were given a rare glimpse of what Western life was all about. As a result of this exposure, several Soviet players started to fight for the right to join the NHL.

Of course, these historical changes have had a far-reaching impact on the NHL. Many of the Soviet pioneers who fought for the right to sign NHL contracts and be given work permits to play in North America were in the prime of their careers when Canada and the USSR faced each other in 1987. Igor Larionov, the center on the legendary KLM line (Krutov-Larionov-Makarov), was one of these pioneers who paved the way for his fellow Russians by battling authorities and voicing his opinion back home.

In an enlightening article written on the occasion of Larionov's 2007 induction into the NHL Hall of Fame, the eminent hockey writer Pierre LeBrun detailed two meetings between Larionov and Wayne Gretzky that happened before Larionov came to the NHL. The first took place during the 1984 Canada Cup, when Gretzky and Larionov discussed the possibility of Soviet players playing in the NHL.

"Back in the '84 Canada Cup," Gretzky recalled, "I got a chance to meet with [Larionov] and spend some time with him. I didn't even know he spoke English. That was the first time I thought maybe those guys might come over and play in the NHL. We talked at length about it."

Then, during the 1987 Canada Cup, Gretzky actually invited the entire Green Unit over to his home in Brantford, Ontario, for a barbecue. The Green Unit was the name of the five-man unit that the Soviet National Team often deployed on the ice at the same time; it consisted of Larionov, Vladimir Krutov, Sergei Makarov, Viacheslav Fetisov and Alexei Kasatonov. The Soviet players went to the barbecue and, though supervised by their ball-breaking coach Viktor Tikhonov, the visit furthered Gretzky's impression that having Russians in the NHL was only a matter of time:

> *That's when I got to know [Larionov] even better, and I found out a lot of those guys wanted to come over and play in the NHL. Both Igor and Fetisov spoke perfect English. Those two guys were the big leaders of trying to get Soviet players over here.*

Meanwhile, back in Moscow, while Gretzky and the Soviets were hamming it up in Brantford, Ovechkin was just discovering the game of hockey. Despite inheriting tremendously athletic genes from his parents—his mother had been an Olympic basketball star, while his father had been a soccer player—neither of them had played much hockey. Their son, Alex, though, picked hockey by instinct. At the age of two, while horsing around in a Soviet toy store, he grabbed a toy hockey stick, a puck and a helmet, and when it was time to go, he refused to give the hockey equipment back. Eventually, his mother bought Alex his first hockey kit.

While Alex was busy learning to walk and working on his shot at home in Moscow, his future hero Mario Lemieux was busy turning himself into a national hero in Canada at the 1987 Canada Cup. All three games in the best-of-three final ended 6–5, and all three games were free-flowing, wide-open affairs, which allowed the greatness on both sides to shine through. It was beautiful hockey to watch, and it reminded the world that there is no greater hockey spectacle than when Canada and Russia collide. Looking back, it is shocking to think three games that ended 6–5 were brilliantly played. But it truly was phenomenal hockey.

The first two games were decided in over-time, with the USSR taking the first game and Canada taking the second. In the decisive final game, with the score knotted once again at five late in the third period, things looked to be heading for an extra frame. But with just over a minute to play and a faceoff deep in the Canadian zone, Dale Hawerchuk won the defensive zone faceoff, and then Mario Lemieux managed to chip the puck out of the zone past a pinching Soviet defender. At center ice, Gretzky picked up the loose puck and entered the Soviet zone on the left wing. With Lemieux trailing and Larry Murphy jumping into the play as a second option, Canada had a 3-on-1. Gretzky used Murphy as a decoy before feathering a pass into the slot for Lemieux to skate onto. A right-handed shot, Lemieux picked the puck up, waltzed towards the goal and snapped a quick shot into the top right-hand corner of the net over Evgeny Beloshejkin's shoulder. Like Paul Henderson's series-clinching goal in the final game of the 1972 Summit Series, Lemieux's goal put a dramatic end to a scintillating display of hockey.

As glorious as the '87 Canada Cup was, it took place in a different era in the evolution of the sport. Over the past 22 years, hockey has changed enormously, and many of the changes are reflected in Alex Ovechkin's style and his stature. At 6 feet, 2 inches and 220 pounds, he is a much bigger physical specimen than the average player in the wide-open era of the 1980s. Unless he was a fighter, it was rare for a player to exceed 200 pounds. Today, most players are in the neighborhood of 200 pounds, and virtually no one plays at 170 to 180 pounds, as Gretzky and Larionov did.

Ovechkin and his generation of Russian stars are also reminding hockey fans how blessed the NHL is to have merged the Canadian brand of hockey with the Russian style of play. As a result of the increased talent pool, there is much greater parity in today's NHL, and there is no question that, in general, the tremendous influx of Russian talent has contributed greatly to the improved caliber of play.

In the 20 years since Russian players first joined the NHL, the game of hockey has also evolved from both a technical and a technological standpoint. Coaching strategies have become far more complex, while the drastic increase in television coverage has allowed teams and players to dissect game footage in the video room. Along with the greater size and speed of NHL players, these technical changes have meant there is less room on the ice for gifted players to weave their magic.

On the other hand, there is the potential for dehumanization when technology and strategy play too central a role in a game that should be based on fun and aesthetic beauty. In the latter half of the 1990s and the early 2000s, we saw that the trap system, infamously employed by the New Jersey Devils, the Dallas Stars and others, had the adverse effect of turning coaches into stars. For several years, the Stanley Cup was carried home by the team that was the most effective in clogging the neutral zone and frustrating its opponents into turning the puck over. Compared to the exciting brand of offensive hockey that ruled in the 1980s, the late '90s was a dreary period in hockey history dominated by defensive systems.

Fortunately, the post-lockout era is returning to beautiful offensive hockey. Thanks in large part to a few strategic rule changes designed to cut down on the clutching and grabbing that enabled mediocre teams to stay competitive, the NHL seems to be evolving into an offensive league once again. In the last two years, the Detroit Red Wings and the Pittsburgh Penguins, two supremely talented teams, have each won the Stanley Cup. From an individual perspective, we are also seeing higher goal and point totals. In 2007–08, Alex Ovechkin became the first player to hit the 60-goal mark since Mario Lemieux and Jaromir Jagr both accomplished the feat 12 years earlier.

Because of these changes, Alexander Ovechkin is the prototype of what a dominant hockey player looks like in today's game. He is big, fast and tough. But, perhaps most significantly, Ovechkin's charisma and charm have been a revelation to many hockey fans.

If we look beyond his many awards and achievements, Ovechkin has rejuvenated the league. Not since Pavel Bure has the NHL seen a player capable of bringing fans out of their seats every time he touches the puck. Like Bure,

Ovechkin also has a magnetic quality to his character that makes it very difficult not to cheer for him. Because he plays with such reckless enthusiasm, he reminds all of us what it felt like to play sports when we were young and having fun.

Chapter One

The Ovechkin Family

Hockey is a bit like theater in a way. Every time there is a line change, it's like a change of decoration or new actors in a theatrical play. The story is going to go another way. Then, of course, it will change again. There is always a plot to the story of a game, shifting characters and action. There is a beauty to it. Somebody is always trying to make a masterpiece out of it. You sit there and wait for that to happen.

–Mikhail Ovechkin, Alexander's father

To me, hockey is less like theater and more like war. You come out five soldiers against five enemy soldiers. You are trying to defeat them and take what they think is theirs.

–Alexander Ovechkin

Alexander Ovechkin was created from unique bloodlines. His mother is Tatiana Ovechkina, one of the greatest female basketball players the sport has ever seen. His father is Mikhail Ovechkin, a former soccer player who was about to turn professional when a torn thigh muscle ended his career prematurely. Sergei, Alexander's older brother, who died in a car wreck, was a wrestler. But Alex Ovechkin is a hockey player. Despite not having any family history with the game, he plays hockey like no one else. Blessed with raw power, reckless athleticism and piercing vision, Ovechkin comes from a strong family, and to know where his ferocity and charisma come from, it is first necessary to know a little something about his parents.

Back in 2004, when Alex Ovechkin was 19 years old and dominating the Russian Super League during the NHL lockout, George McPhee, general manager of the Washington Capitals, went to Moscow to check out his stud prospect. After the game, the Ovechkin family invited McPhee, along with Gleb Chistyakov, the Capitals' chief Russian scout, back to their home for dinner.

Russians are known for their hospitality, and unlike the American-style rapid-fire dinner, Russian dinners are often prolonged affairs that feature several courses and multiple toasts, which of course means multiple shots of vodka. Here is how George McPhee described the evening he and Gleb Chistyakov spent with the Ovechkins:

> *We spent a wonderful evening there. They could not have been more genuine, warm, loving people. We arrived, and they told us to get out of our business suits and provided us with sweats and told us to relax. We took saunas, went swimming, then had about a three-hour dinner with the family. Mr. Ovechkin toasted us, then about 30 minutes later, Mrs. Ovechkin toasted us, and both welcomed us to their home.*

Tatiana Ovechkina: The Mother

Many moons ago, and long before Alex was born, a seven-year-old girl named Tatiana Kabayeya was walking home from school with some friends through the streets of Moscow. It was 1957, and things were about to turn bad for little Tatiana. While walking, she was struck by a passing car, and her right leg took the brunt of the impact. Her leg was badly damaged in the accident, and the recovery was downright brutal.

In a 2006 article for the *Washington Post*, April Witt described the aftermath of the accident:

> *Her right leg was so mangled that doctors initially wanted to amputate. Instead, Tatiana*

Kabayeya spent a year in a Moscow hospital, her leg suspended in traction. When her shinbone failed to mend properly, doctors re-broke it three times.

To this day, Tatiana still has a massive scar that stretches from just above her right ankle to the middle of her thigh.

Both of Tatiana's legs had atrophied after spending a year in the hospital waiting for her right leg to heal. Her legs were so weak after her release from hospital that she had to wear thick boots to protect her legs from further injury. She was forbidden to play sports or do anything that might stress her fragile limbs. Naturally, it was a humiliating experience for an eight-year-old girl.

During this period of rest and recovery, Tatiana's older sister was busy playing basketball in the Dynamo children's league. (For more information on the Dynamo Sports Club—how it functions and its history—please see Chapter Two.) Tatiana occasionally tagged along, and one day, the Dynamo coach tossed Tatiana a ball and invited her to take a shot. And that was it—Tatiana was hooked. From that point on, she became obsessed with making the Dynamo team.

Over the next few months, she used bricks as weights and gradually built up the strength in her legs. Without the modern convenience of a local gym around the corner, Tatiana worked out the old-fashioned way. Every day, she sat behind her family's apartment building and put bricks in a plastic bag that she would hook around her leg and do leg lifts. After both legs could handle one brick, she added another and then another. Slowly but surely, her legs got stronger and so did her determination.

"It sounds primitive," Tatiana once said about her training regimen, "but you had to understand I had no advice. I had to make things up myself. I don't remember how many bricks I worked up to. I loved basketball so much that I worked until I was beside myself. I would train until I was out of my mind."

By the time she was 16, Tatiana had been through more adversity than most athletes deal with in a lifetime. But through bull-headed determination and her desire to play basketball, she carved out a spot for herself on the Dynamo team. She was a 5-foot 8-inch point guard, and it didn't take her long to blossom into the team's star and captain.

By the age of 19, Tatiana was also the starting point guard and captain of the supremely talented Soviet national team. As the point guard, her role was to get the ball inside to the Soviet's primary scoring threat, a 7-foot 2-inch center by the name of Juliana Semenova. At the dawn of women's basketball, Tatiana and Semenova were like Stockton and Malone, a dynamic duo that other teams could not stop even though they knew exactly what was coming.

At the 1976 Summer Olympics in Montréal, women's basketball was an Olympic sport for the first time, and the Soviets destroyed their competition. In their semifinal game against the United States, they annihilated the Americans by a score of 112–77. The next Summer Olympics took place in the Ovechkins' hometown of Moscow, and with many countries boycotting the 1980 Games, including the United States, Tatiana and her Soviet teammates repeated as Olympic champions. "To win in the Olympics," Tatiana once said, "is the biggest reward for any athlete."

During her stellar career, Tatiana also won the 1975 World Championship and six European Championships (1970, 1972, 1974, 1976, 1978, 1980). In fact, while she was on the Soviet national team, the team never lost a single game in an official international competition.

When her playing days were over, Tatiana remained heavily involved in Russian basketball. After she retired as a player, she quickly took over the reins of the program that had trained her from the time she was nine years old. For two years, she coached the Dynamo women's basketball team, and since then, she has served as the club's president.

Mikhail Ovechkin: The Father

Before the Bolshevik Revolution of 1919, Alexander Ovechkin's paternal great-grandfather was the owner of a bread factory just outside the Moscow city center. After the post-revolutionary purges, the Ovechkin clan moved into the city, where three families shared a two-room apartment. Twelve people were crammed into what would now be considered a bachelor pad. This was Mikhail Ovechkin's first home.

By the time he was nine, Mikhail and his family were able to move into a flat of their own. It was in the same neighborhood as the stadium where the Dynamo soccer team played, and young Mikhail was an avid soccer fan and a pretty good player, too. Like his wife, Mikhail spent his adolescence in the Dynamo training system, which, in the old Soviet regime, was gruelingly militaristic. Of course, it was better than being in the military, because you were playing sports, but even athletes weren't given a whole lot of freedom in their daily schedules. By and large, they lived in barracks, were told where and when to eat and were told how many hours to train.

During his teens, Mikhail Ovechkin was a gifted soccer player who moved through the Dynamo junior ranks and was en route to becoming a professional soccer player—until he shredded his thigh. At 17, Mikhail had just signed a professional contract to play soccer for the Dynamo men's team. But the torn thigh muscle ended any hope of playing soccer long term, and so he moved on. A year later, Mikhail was waiting for a train outside the Dynamo Moscow station when he met Tatiana. She was 19 and just hitting her basketball prime. Mikhail, on the other hand, spent his time driving a taxi around the streets of Moscow. Looking at Mikhail, he is a big teddy bear of a man. He is kind, outgoing and very insightful. Like his wife, he speaks English only in fragments, but it is not hard to imagine that in his native tongue, he is a skillful storyteller.

As young adults, Mikhail and Tatiana were lucky to be able to see each other. At the time, Tatiana and her teammates lived in training barracks. Even married women were not allowed to live with their husbands. But somehow, Tatiana and Mikhail received a special allowance from the Dynamo authorities, and they were permitted to share a room.

Throughout the 1970s, Tatiana played basketball, and Mikhail drove a cab. By the time the

1990s hit and the Soviet Union collapsed, Russia was left in dire economic straits. Like many other non-essential things in Russian life at the time, the women's basketball program at Dynamo was in jeopardy. Fortunately, Mikhail's many years as a cab driver listening to clients had taught him a thing or two. "Cabbies know everything," he once said when asked about his role in saving the women's basketball program at Dynamo. "Cabbies know people who leave big tips." In other words, Mikhail had contacts. Eventually, these contacts were able to sponsor the Dynamo women's basketball program, keeping it afloat.

Given Mikhail's role in securing some much-needed financial assistance, the club offered him a position with Tatiana's team. With a young family to raise, the Ovechkins now had a modicum of financial stability during a period in Russian history when many people throughout the broken state lacked basic necessities and faced the threat of starvation.

Sergei Ovechkin: The Eldest Brother

Sadly, Sergei Ovechkin died at the age of 22. When Alex, Tatiana and Mikhail are asked about Sergei, they all prefer to talk about other subjects. In keeping with the family's desire to leave the matter private, let's move on.

Mikhail Ovechkin: The Other Older Brother

Unlike his flashy brother, Alex, Mikhail Ovechkin is like the majority of young men in the world who are plugging away at life, just trying to make ends meet. When he first came to the U.S. with Alex and their parents, Mikhail's main work experience back home had been with the Moscow Dynamo women's basketball team, where he had spent six years touring Europe with the team.

When Alex moved to Washington in 2005, the entire family came with him, including Mikhail. During his rookie year, Alex bought a $1.5-million mansion in Arlington, Virginia, and the two brothers lived together while Mikhail tried to line up some work. Eventually, he landed a job as the manager of team operations on the staff of the Washington Mystics, a women's basketball team that plays in the WNBA (Women's National Basketball Association).

For Mikhail, it must be a strange thing to be the low-profile brother of a stud hockey star. In North America, where sports stars are treated like gods, revered for their unearthly and enviable abilities, Mikhail lives a good life, but he is not a star. He smokes Marlboro cigarettes; he has a live-in girlfriend named Lauren; and he analyzes videotapes of the Mystics games, looking to isolate trends, bad habits, mistakes and good plays. Like most sports in the modern era, having someone competent behind the scenes to break down video is an indispensable aspect of the coaching process. This is what Mikhail Ovechkin does. He has a keen eye for detail, and instead of being center stage in every arena he enters, Mikhail's work takes place in a small room where he sits alone with a TV and a remote control.

In a 2008 article for the *Washington Times*, Harlan Goode wrote a profile of Mikhail entitled "The District's Other Ovechkin." The article portrayed Mikhail in the following way:

> *He stands just outside the entrance to Verizon Center, Marlboro in one hand, iPhone in the other. He stares straight ahead, exchanging brief glances with passersby.*

> *Do they recognize him? Do they see the similarity—the wide face, the way his eyebrows run together? Do they know that this short, soft-bellied man with the tousled hair and the five-o'clock shadow is but a few strands of DNA removed from the greatest hockey player on the planet?*

> *No, they pass him by, barely acknowledging his existence as he flicks the cigarette butt*

into the street, stamps it out and lights another. Got to get that second one in quick before halftime ends. He takes two deep drags, then glances at his phone.

"Time to go," Mikhail Ovechkin says through a thick Russian accent. "Game starts soon."

As Mikhail Ovechkin rushes back to his job, there isn't a hint of the luxurious lifestyle that his brother leads. There is no flashy sports car. There are no supermodel girlfriends. There are no paparazzi angling for shots, no Dolce & Gabbana to strut around in and no kids hunting for signatures. Of course, Mikhail will tell you that he feels no jealousy towards his brother's fame and success. But this is the American Dream we're talking about, and in the United States, where the rich and famous as treated as role models and idols, it would be very difficult to toil through a humble existence without wishing for your share of the pie. After all, the American Dream isn't about finding happiness through hard work—at least not any more. In the 21st century, the American Dream has everything to do with fame and money, and Alexander Ovechkin has plenty of both.

Chapter Two

The Prodigy

Alexander Ovechkin's love affair with hockey began at the tender age of two, while playing in a Soviet toy store called Детский мир ("Children's World"). Sasha, the Russian nickname for Alexander and the name his parents use, grabbed a toy hockey stick, a puck and a helmet, and when it was time to go, he refused to give the hockey equipment back. Eventually, his mother bought the gear, and Alex's persistence got him his first hockey kit.

From that point on, he grew increasingly obsessed with the game, apparently throwing tantrums if his parents tried to change the channel when a game was on TV. Despite his fascination with the sport, it wasn't until he was seven years old that Alex was enrolled in a hockey program. But Alex was growing up during an extremely turbulent period in Russia, and his parents were busy working and had difficulty taking him to his hockey practices. In 1992, when he started playing hockey, the Soviet Union had finally collapsed when Boris Yeltsin led a military coup that overthrew the Gorbachev administration and its perestroika (rebuilding) program that was designed to shift away from communism gradually.

Of course, the Soviet system had been disintegrating for the better part of a decade, but the final collapse in 1991 meant that a communist government no longer provided its citizens with the basic necessities of life. After 72 years of communism, it goes without saying that the sudden shift from communism to open-market capitalism brought chaos and strife to Russian life. Not that there hadn't been major problems before, but the 1990s was a time of intense poverty throughout Russia.

One of the offshoots of the change was that Russia's vast natural resources hit the open market and were seized by whoever had the ambition to exploit them. Although a small percentage of Russians began capitalizing on the new social reality and building stunning fortunes, the vast majority struggled to put food on the table.

In the Ovechkin household, the transition would have been stark. Because Tatiana was a recognized athlete who had served the motherland by winning consecutive Olympic gold medals in 1976 and 1980, her family would have been handsomely supported by the state. Despite the erosion of the country's infrastructure during the 1980s, the Ovechkins would have lived very comfortably during the Soviet era.

But by 1992, whatever vestiges of government infrastructure that remained were more or less dysfunctional. In essence, this meant the average Russian family, instead of serving the state in exchange for basic necessities, was now in an all-out struggle for survival. Many areas of Russia lacked electricity and clean drinking water.

Naturally, this historical background has a lot to do with Ovechkin's persistent and relentless character. As a child, he would have had relatively little compared to the lifestyle most North American kids experience. It also would have been fairly common in this early post-Soviet period for kids to dream of the Western lifestyle. Ovechkin, after all, is a part of the first generation of Russians who didn't grow up under a Soviet regime. During the difficult period of transition in which education was overhauled and poverty ran rampant, kids were being exposed to the Western way of life—and for the most part, American things were seen as "cool" because they were associated with visions and dreams of a better life.

Of course, when he started playing hockey as a seven-year-old kid, the young Alexander was a long way away from dreaming of the NHL and hoisting the Stanley Cup over his head. In the early 1990s, information and news from the Western world were just beginning to enter Russia. By the time he was a teenager, though, Ovechkin had received enough stories about the NHL to be a fan of Mario Lemieux and Owen Nolan. Lemieux was, of course, the biggest star in the NHL in the early '90s—he was putting up Gretzky-like numbers with regularity and he won two Stanley Cups as a player in 1991 and 1992. Owen Nolan's heyday came a little later, and it was his robust style that caught Ovechkin's attention.

The Tragic Passing of Sergei Ovechkin

There is one topic Alex Ovechkin does not like to discuss. Although he doesn't get angry when a reporter asks him about his older brother, he just says he doesn't want to talk about it. Given his willingness to broach nearly any other subject, though, you can't help but respect his wish to keep this part of his life private.

For the sake of honoring the influence Sergei had on his younger brother, the one story we have is that Sergei was instrumental in keeping Alex in the game of hockey. After Alex played a little bit in a hockey school at the age of seven, his parents were having difficulty getting him to and from practices. His coaches, however, made it clear that despite his limited experience on the ice, Alex had a special talent for the game. It was Sergei, though, who forced the issue at home and fought to keep his brother playing hockey. Between the ages of eight and 10, Alex moved quickly through the ranks of the Dynamo youth hockey program.

Sadly, just as Alexander's hockey was beginning to thrive with the regularity of playing in an elite program, his older brother died in a car crash. Sergei Ovechkin, who had been developing into a terrific wrestler, was just 22.

"He is my idol," Alex has said about his older brother. "At that moment [when Sergei died], I realized life is that—when it's gone it's gone. You can't get it back. You have to take from life what you can."

True to his word, Alex Ovechkin has pushed the envelope and seized every opportunity the game of hockey has afforded him. Prior to the 2004 NHL Entry Draft when Washington drafted

Ovechkin with the first overall selection, one scout
had this assessment of the 18-year-old Ovechkin:

> *I think everyone likes what they see on the
> ice, but the off-ice person seems to be the type
> of player that everybody covets. He's a real
> driven guy that wants to be as good as he
> can be. I've never heard any negative com-
> ments about his character. Everybody
> thinks this is the complete guy in terms of
> not only skill level and talent, but also
> determination and drive to be as good as
> he can be.*

Since his entry into the NHL, Ovechkin has
fulfilled his tremendous promise as both a player
and as a person. He scores goals, thrills fans, hits
like a ton of bricks, back checks, never gives up
on a play and inspires teammates and fans alike.
Off the ice, he embraces fans and welcomes
media interviews, and he loves to put on a show
when the occasion calls for it. Simply put, can
you think of any other athlete who takes more
from life than Alexander Ovechkin?

Moscow Dynamo

The Dynamo Sports Club is the oldest sports
club in Russia. It was created in 1923, long before
hockey was being played in the Soviet Union.
At that time, which was four years after the

Russian Revolution and in the early days of the Soviet Union, the Dynamo Sports Club was sponsored by the State Political Directorate—the original Soviet political police that evolved into the more notorious state security apparatus of the KGB. In 1937, the Dynamo sports society won the Order of Lenin, which was awarded annually to exceptional citizens or organizations that provided exemplary service to the state.

In the Soviet Union, hockey boomed in popularity immediately after World War II. In 1946, HC Dynamo Moscow, the hockey branch of the Dynamo Sports Club, was founded and sponsored by the KGB. By 1971, the Dynamo club was practicing 45 sports disciplines, including hockey, basketball, football (soccer) and volleyball. Among the more recognizable names the Dynamo Sports Club trained were Alexander Maltsev (hockey), Lev Yashin (hockey and football) and, most interestingly, Tatiana Ovechkina (basketball), Alexander Ovechkin's mother.

Like his mother, Alex Ovechkin was trained in the Dynamo Sports Club, and because there are no elite junior ranks like the Canadian Hockey League (CHL) for young Russians to hone their craft, Ovechkin began playing professional hockey as a 16-year-old with Moscow Dynamo.

As a young boy growing up in Moscow, Ovechkin's hockey hero was Alexander Maltsev, who was one of the few Soviet-era stars not to play for CSKA Moscow, the team run by the Soviet Army. Maltsev was a fixture on the national team, and he played at the club level for Dynamo. Although Maltsev retired from the professional ranks in 1984, the year before Ovechkin was born, Ovechkin developed an admiration for Maltsev through stories, legends and TV highlights. Maltsev was, it should be mentioned, one of the greatest offensive players the Soviet Union had produced, and given the Ovechkin family's long ties to Dynamo, it is hardly surprising that Ovechkin idolized Maltsev.

Beginning in the Soviet era, the developmental system for Russian players has always been based on fostering a long-term relationship between a young player and the club that finds or claims him. In Ovechkin's case, all of his hockey training was with Dynamo's youth hockey program.

At the age of 16, when most players are still slowly climbing through the junior ranks, Ovechkin made his debut for Moscow Dynamo. In 21 games at the tail end of the 2001–02 season, he scored two goals and added two assists. With this brief experience of professional hockey in his back pocket, Ovechkin then played in his first major international tournament for Russia at the 2002 Under-18 World Championships. Although Russia came up short in the final against the United States, Ovechkin dominated the tournament by scoring 14 goals in only eight games (8-14-4-18).

Over the next two seasons, Ovechkin's play in the Russian Super League (RSL) steadily improved as his body filled out and he adjusted to the pace of professional hockey. In his third year in the RSL, Ovechkin was only 18 years old, but he was already one of the league's best players. Although HC Dynamo Moscow didn't have much playoff success during Ovechkin's first three years, fate conspired to bring him back for a fourth year.

After being drafted into the NHL by the Washington Capitals in 2004, the NHL lockout happened, and the entire 2004–05 NHL season was lost. During this yearlong labor dispute, many NHL players took the opportunity to play in other professional leagues throughout Europe, and the bulk of them went to Russia. Naturally, Ovechkin played for Dynamo, and it was his best season. Although he missed two months of the season with a shoulder injury he had sustained while playing in that year's gold-medal game against Canada at the World Junior Championships (which Canada won 6–1), Ovechkin recovered from his injury and returned to Dynamo with a vengeance. Throughout the season, Ovechkin played on the top line, and at the end of the year, he was named the RSL's best left-winger. In a league that only gives one assist on goals, Ovechkin put up 27 points in 37 games (37-13-14-27) and then added another six points in 10 games (10-2-4-6) while helping Dynamo capture its first Russian Championship in five years.

The 2003 and 2004 IIHF World Junior Championships

From a North American perspective, because Russian hockey is pretty much off the radar, the annual World Junior Championships (an Under-20 tournament) during the Christmas holidays are where NHL fans often get their first glimpse of up-and-coming talent. In 2003, the World Junior Championships took place in the Nova Scotia, and although Canada was favored (as usual) to win, many savvy hockey observers had their eye on a 16-year-old Russian phenom by the name of Alexander Ovechkin. Despite being a year younger than most of his competition, Ovechkin played a starring role for the Russians that year by scoring six goals in six games (6-6-1-7). As is often the case in international hockey, Russia and Canada breezed through the round-robin stage and won their semifinal games to set up a dream final between the two powerhouses of the hockey world.

Although Ovechkin didn't score in the final, Russia managed to overcome a 2–1 deficit to beat Canada 3–2 in an extremely well-played final. The final also set a TSN record for the largest audience in the network's 19-year history. The live broadcast aired on January 6, 2003, and it drew an average audience of 3,446,000 viewers. At the peak of the game, during the final 30 minutes, TSN had over four million viewers.

The following year, Ovechkin once again proved to the hockey world that he was a dominant force. His team, however, was much weaker than in previous years, despite the added presence of Evgeni Malkin. Malkin and Ovechkin played well on Russia's top line, each averaging a point per game, but Russia finished the tournament with a disappointing fifth-place finish.

The Florida Panthers Select Alexander Ovechkin

In the NHL, draft eligibility works as follows: if you have already turned 18 by September 15 and you are no older than 20 by December 31, you are eligible for the following year's draft, which takes place in June. As it happens, Alex Ovechkin's birthday is September 17, 1985, which means that he fell two days' short of being eligible for the 2003 entry draft. The Florida Panthers, however, tried their damnedest to get Ovechkin ahead of schedule.

Prior to the 2003 NHL draft, Florida general manager Rick Dudley had petitioned the NHL authorities a few times, claiming that Ovechkin could be eligible if they took into account the four leap years that had occurred since his birth. Eventually, the NHL conceded that Dudley had a point, and they agreed to let the Panthers use their ninth-round pick to select Ovechkin. Upon further review, though, the league ruled the selection invalid. Florida got their ninth-round pick back, and with it, they selected Tanner Glass, a minor-league plumber who has just earned a contract with the Vancouver Canucks after an impressive prospects camp. But can you imagine how much less Florida would suck if they had managed to steal Ovechkin in 2003?

In an interesting parallel, Dudley's clever ploy to draft Ovechkin a year ahead of his apparent eligibility has a precedent. Back in 1989, when the first wave of Soviet players was coming to the NHL, one of the hottest Soviet prospects was Pavel Bure. However, given the newness of Soviet players in the NHL and the uncertainty of being able to work out a transfer agreement with the Soviet League, few teams were willing to risk wasting an early-round draft pick on a Soviet prospect.

In 1989, although Bure was 18 years old and eligible to be drafted in the first three rounds, an old stipulation set certain guidelines regarding playing experience during the later rounds. According to NHL rules at the time, in order to be drafted after the third round, Soviet players had to have played at least two seasons (with a minimum of 11 games per season) with the professional club that held their rights in Europe. Since Bure hadn't played the 11 required games in one of his seasons with CSKA Moscow, he was thought to be ineligible.

But the Canucks' head scout at the time, Mike Penny, discovered that Bure had played in a few other exhibition and international games than were on his official record—a fact that, if true, made him eligible. Vancouver drafted Bure in the sixth round, and although the pick was originally deemed illegal by league president John Ziegler, the Canucks (with the help of Igor Larionov) were able to secure documents proving that Bure had played in other games, and on the eve of the 1990 NHL draft, Vancouver's draft pick was accepted.

The Ovechkin Sweepstakes

Because the Florida Panthers' attempt to draft Ovechkin was denied by league officials, Ovechkin was the clear-cut favorite to be drafted first over-all in the 2004 draft. In fact, he was so clearly the type of player you could build a franchise around that if he had been eligible for the 2003 draft, he likely would have been chosen number one ahead of other highly touted prospects, such as Marc-André Fleury, Nathan Horton and Eric Staal. In the end, the Pittsburgh Penguins, who held the number one pick, selected Marc-André Fleury, who is now blossoming into an elite goal-tender, with a Stanley Cup on his resume after Pittsburgh's 2009 triumph.

In any case, with Ovechkin and Evgeni Malkin set to go first and second in the draft, Washington got lucky at the 2004 Draft Lottery. Each year, the 14 teams that miss the playoffs are part of a lot-tery to determine the draft order. The team that finishes dead last (in 2003–04, it was Pittsburgh) gets 25 percent of the balls in the lottery. Signifi-cantly, teams can only move up by a maximum of four spots, which means only the bottom five teams have a shot at getting the first overall pick. Because of the odds, the team that finishes last (in this case, Pittsburgh) has a 48.1 percent chance of selecting first, while the second-to-last team (Chicago) has an 18.8 percent chance, and the third worst team (Washington) has a 14.2 percent shot. At the 2004 Draft Lottery, however, the stars aligned in Washington's favor, and they took Alexander Ovechkin.

As a junior-age prospect, Ovechkin had been compared to the best prospects the hockey world had ever seen. In Russia, he was the most highly touted prospect since Vladimir Krutov and Sergei Makarov. In North America, many scouts were claiming he was the best thing to come along since Mario Lemieux, who had been drafted in the number-one slot in 1984, 20 years earlier.

Already an imposing figure at 6 feet 2 inches and 214 pounds, Ovechkin had even played for Team Russia as a 17-year-old at the 2004 World Cup of Hockey. He was the first junior-age Russian to be named to the senior men's team since legendary goaltender Vladislav Tretiak had played for the Soviet Union 35 years earlier.

Chapter Three

Ovechkin the Conqueror

*The media attention doesn't affect him.
How can I put this? He came to conquer
America. With the help of the guys on his
team, he will conquer the United States.
And it is not a bad thing to be Russian and
to be recognized on the street.*

–Mikhail Ovechkin, Alexander's father

The Ovechkin Philosophy

A few weeks before the 2004 draft, Ovechkin was asked if he cared about being drafted number one. "I want to be number one because I always want to be number one. If I play, I want to be number one. If I'm drafted, I want to be number one. Always number one." As a statement about Ovechkin's character, it is honest, straightforward and sincere. Of course, there is nothing particularly diplomatic about it, but this is precisely what everyone loves about Ovechkin.

Unlike Sidney Crosby, who has been trained to fend off the media by being polite and diplomatic, Ovechkin never seems to concern himself with how the media might portray him. As a result, he comes across as a brash and supremely confident young man who expresses whatever his instinct compels him to express. When he plays, he plays like a man possessed by the desire to have fun, the drive to score goals and the determination to win hockey games.

When he speaks, although his English is a work in progress, he always manages to express sincere emotions and ideas. Depending on his mood and the situation, he can be hilarious or profane, colloquial or formal; and he can convey the thrill of victory or the agony of defeat by just the look on his face.

A Brief History of the Washington Capitals

Prior to drafting Alexander Ovechkin with the first overall pick in the 2004 NHL Entry Draft, the Washington Capitals had spent most of their 20-year history alternating between mediocrity and brutality. Back in 1974–75, the NHL expanded by adding the Washington Capitals, the New York Islanders, the Atlanta Flames and the Kansas City Scouts. Unfortunately for the newcomers, they had entered the league at a messy juncture in NHL history.

Throughout the 1970s, hockey underwent something of a cold war in which players wanted more money, and owners wanted to keep their growing profits to themselves. The fundamental offshoot of these tensions was that a new league was formed that set out to rival the NHL. The inaugural season of the World Hockey Association (WHA) was 1972, by which time 67 NHL players had jumped ship to join the new league, including Bobby Hull, who was one of the NHL's biggest stars at the time. Hull signed a massive multi-year contract with the Winnipeg Jets for $250,000 per year. The contract also included a $1-million signing bonus. Back then, it was by far the most lucrative contract in hockey history.

According to hockey lore, Hull had been threatening to move to the WHA as part of a negotiation tactic designed to get more money out of the Chicago Blackhawks. When asked by a reporter if he would really go to the upstart league, Hull joked that he would only go for a million dollars, which was a ludicrous amount of money then. The average NHL salary, after all, was a measly $25,000. But wouldn't you know it, the Winnipeg Jets landed the Golden Jet by offering him a million-dollar contract.

Another interesting development during the turbulent WHA era was that most of the WHA teams had filled out their rosters by signing a few European players. Much to the surprise of most North Americans, it eventually became clear that Europeans could play the North American brand of hockey. This development was the first real challenge to the common view that Europeans, though talented, were unsuited to the North American game.

But let's get back to the Washington Capitals. It was during this standoff between the NHL and the WHA that the Capitals came into existence. But the 10 new franchises that formed the WHA had an extremely thin talent pool from which to build. In Washington's case, they were particularly inept at finding good talent. In their first season, they set the bar lower than any other team in NHL history by going 8-67-5. The eight wins are still the fewest in the modern era, while their 0.131 winning percentage is the lowest in NHL history.

Throughout the 1970s, Washington remained a perennial bottom-feeder. Finally, after nearly a decade of missing the playoffs, the Caps made their playoff debut in 1983 on the strength of a potent offense and a stable defense. Their roster throughout much of the 1980s included the likes of Rod Langway, Scott Stevens, Kevin Hatcher, Bobby Carpenter, Dennis Maruk, Mike Gartner, Dave Christian and Dino Ciccarelli. After the regular-season futility that had plagued the Caps during their first decade of existence, their second decade was largely defined by playoff futility. Like the San Jose Sharks in recent times, the Washington Capitals of the 1980s were often a powerhouse during the regular season but blew it in the playoffs. Despite 14 consecutive playoff appearances between 1983 and 1996, Washington was knocked out of the playoffs in their first or second round eight years in a row.

During the late 1990s, after a few down seasons, Washington returned to NHL prominence. In 1998, with a team that featured Peter Bondra, Adam Oates, Dale Hunter, Sergei Gonchar and Olaf Kolzig, the Capitals reached their first Stanley Cup final in franchise history. Although they were swept by the Detroit Red Wings in four straight games, it had been a Cinderella run to remember for Washington fans.

On the heels of this surprise Stanley Cup run, the Capitals flirted with greatness for the next few seasons. They won back-to-back Southeast Division titles in 2000 and 2001 but were eliminated in the playoffs both seasons by the

Pittsburgh Penguins, who have been a nemesis since the Penguin teams of the 1990s that always featured Mario Lemieux. Although the Caps tried to gain the upper hand on their bitter rival by trading for Jaromir Jagr in the summer of 2001, and then signing Robert Lang in the summer of 2002, the two Czech stars and former Penguin teammates never really rekindled the chemistry they had had in Pittsburgh at the tail end of the '90s.

As a result of the repeated playoff failures, Washington gutted their team over the course of the 2003–04 season. Despite his status as a legend, Jagr was by then an underperforming, second-tier talent with an outrageous $11-million salary, which made him difficult to move. In the end, he was traded to the New York Rangers for Anson Carter and an agreement that Washington would pick up $4 million of his salary. After that, the floodgates opened, and all of Washington's high-priced talent was shipped out. Bondra was traded to Ottawa, Gonchar went to Boston and Lang, despite being the league's leading scorer at the time, was sent to Detroit. Washington finished the year with a horrendous record of 23-46-10-6, good for second-last place in the league along with the Chicago Blackhawks. But during the off-season, the Capitals' luck changed when they won the draft lottery, giving them the right to select Alexander Ovechkin. And the rest, as they say, is history.

After playing the lockout season of 2004–05 in Moscow, where he led Dynamo to the RSL Championship, Ovechkin made his NHL debut in 2005–06. For hockey fans who had suffered through the trials and tribulations of a lost season during which they were forced to replace NHL hockey with curling, figure skating and junior level hockey—and more Michael Landsberg than any TV viewer should have to stomach—the NHL was welcomed back like a long-lost friend.

During the lockout, hockey fans will no doubt recall the pain and misery of endless news cycles as our beloved sports networks struggled to fill our ravenous need for hockey news. But with little progress in the collective-bargaining war, no highlight reels to show and no trades or rumors to report, analysts speculated endlessly that the NHL and its players were running the risk of alienating their fans. But as pundits and prognosticators wondered for the sake of debate whether or not fans would hold a grudge, what actually happened was that the absence made the fans' hearts grow fonder. Or, if you look at the situation from a more skeptical perspective, we could also say that the things we wasted our time on when hockey went away made us collectively realize how desperately obsessed we are with the sport. Either way you slice it, when hockey returned with a heavenly crop of rookies highlighted by Alexander Ovechkin and Sidney Crosby, hockey fans welcomed our heroes and villains back with open arms.

The 2005–06 Season

By the time Ovechkin made his NHL debut on October 5, 2005, he was 20 years old and had played three full seasons against men in the Russian Super League. It is little wonder, then, that he had no trouble adjusting to the NHL. In his first NHL game, Ovechkin put his full arsenal on display in helping the Capitals eke out a 3–2 win over the Columbus Blue Jackets. During the game, he threw his weight around and scored two goals. In an ESPN post-game report, Ovechkin's performance was summarized in these terms:

> *His first NHL check was so fierce it dislodged a support beam. He refused to let his team lose, twice answering with goals less than 90 seconds after the opponents took the lead. And when his face appeared on the large scoreboard, he stuck out his tongue and flashed a charismatic smile. After the game, when asked how the win felt, Ovechkin had this to say: "I feel my dreams come true. I play in NHL. First game,*

we win…. We win this game, and I scored the goals. And I'm very happy."

From that point on, Ovechkin tore the league to shreds. He started the year on an eight-game point-scoring streak, and he never really looked back. En route to winning the Calder Trophy as Rookie of the Year, Ovechkin put up spectacular numbers. In 81 games, he scored 52 goals and added 54 assists (81-52-54-106). So electric was he that if he'd had a better supporting cast, he surely would have garnered MVP consideration. Instead, Washington missed the playoffs despite the fact that Ovechkin finished third in league scoring behind only Joe Thornton and Jaromir Jagr.

Over the course of the 2005–06 season, the comparisons between Sidney Crosby and Ovechkin were inevitable. Both had been highly touted prospects for a few years, and although Ovechkin was highly regarded, Crosby initially drew more hype. In part, this had to do with Crosby being Canadian and the Canadian need to label someone "the next Gretzky." And Crosby fit the bill. Like Gretzky, Crosby is a diplomatic player with tremendous imagination and vision on the ice. He has soft hands, a scoring touch, miraculous passing skills and an intense drive to succeed. And although Ovechkin has become even more popular than Crosby over time, in their rookie seasons, all eyes were on Crosby.

Despite being two years younger than Ovechkin in his rookie season, Crosby kept pace with Ovechkin by scoring 39 goals and 63 assists (81-39-63-102). Crosby also added a surprising 110 penalty minutes, which earned "Sid the Kid" the reputation of being a bit of a whiner who would stand up for himself by resorting to a little stick-work. In any case, Crosby became the first rookie to record 100 points and 100 penalty minutes in a season. At the end of the day, however, Ovechkin took home the hardware. Their statistics were comparable, but Ovechkin's 50-goal, 100-point season marked just the second time an NHL rookie had hit both landmarks—Teemu Selanne had been the first when he potted an astronomical 76 goals and 132 points in his 1992–93 rookie season with the Winnipeg Jets.

In the long-standing debate about which rookie was better, Ovechkin and Crosby both deserved credit for living up to their hype. But when the Calder Trophy was presented, Ovechkin received 124 of the 129 first-place votes and won the Calder in a landslide. Ovechkin was also named a First Team NHL All-Star, and he set a rookie record by shooting on net 425 times, the third highest total in NHL history.

During his inaugural season, Ovechkin's signature moment took place in a game against the Phoenix Coyotes. Although Washington had the game under control, leading 5–1 midway through the third period, "The Goal," as hockey-savvy fans now casually call it, will go down as one of the greatest goals in hockey history, despite its relative unimportance.

After stealing the puck from a Phoenix player in the neutral zone, Ovechkin charged into the Phoenix zone in a one-on-one situation against Phoenix defenseman Paul Mara. As he reached the slot, Mara challenged Ovechkin by getting his gloves into Ovechkin's chest. Ovechkin was thrown off balance by the contact, and as he fell to the ice, his momentum took him through the slot and towards the bottom of the faceoff circle. Despite falling to the ice at full speed and spinning like a corkscrew, Ovechkin stayed with the puck and fully extended his stick over his head. Using the toe of his stick blade, he then managed to sweep the puck towards the goal, and it had enough steam to find the near corner of the open net. The goal became an instant YouTube classic, and Ovechkin celebrated with his trademark left-handed fist pump and a kiss on his glove—a glove that he raises after every goal in honor of his departed brother Sergei.

The 2006 Winter Olympics: Turin, Italy

In the middle of his phenomenal rookie season in the NHL, Ovechkin played for the Russian National Team during the 2006 Olympics. Significantly, Ovechkin's mother won back-to-back Olympic gold medals as the starting point guard and captain of the Soviet women's basketball team—at the 1976 Summer Olympics in Montréal and at the 1980 Games in her native Moscow. Because of his mother's Olympic success, Alex Ovechkin had long dreamed of following in her footsteps by leading his country to Olympic gold.

In the buildup to the Turin Olympics, many hockey pundits believed that Canada and Russia would inevitably face each other in the gold-medal game. But it wasn't meant to be. Neither of the pre-eminent hockey superpowers went home with a medal as Sweden beat Finland in an all-Scandinavia final. Russia, which had eliminated Canada in the quarterfinals, finished fourth, while Canada ended the tournament with a shocking seventh-place finish.

From the Canadian hockey perspective, fans will no doubt recall that the 2006 edition of Team Canada was in disarray from the get-go. Wayne Gretzky, who had been the successful architect behind the Olympic triumph at the 2002 Olympics in Salt Lake City, assembled the 2006 squad.

However, just prior to the Olympics, an incendiary story about an NHL betting scandal broke, and Gretzky found himself at the center of the firestorm. Along with his wife Janet, Rick Tocchet (Gretzky's former assistant coach in Phoenix) and roughly half a dozen NHL players, Gretzky was being accused of playing a role in a gambling ring.

For the NHL, the story surfaced at the worst possible time. The Olympics were to take place only six months after the league had lost the 2005–06 season to a lockout. During the lost year, many new hockey fans lost interest in the sport, and some die-hard fans grew weary of listening to a bunch of millionaires squabbling over money. Fortunately, the return of the NHL featured Sidney Crosby and Alexander Ovechkin, two sure-fire stars who were exciting on the ice and marketable off the ice. In any case, the last thing the NHL needed was a Pete Rose–style story that might threaten the image the NHL was trying to rebuild in the aftermath of the lockout.

For Team Canada, on the other hand, the betting scandal was an annoying distraction at best and a crippling omen at worst. Because it was a juicy story full of intrigue and plot twists, it followed Gretzky to Turin, where the media wove the betting angle into the Olympic effort.

Will Team Canada be distracted by Gretzky's presence? Should Gretzky have stayed home? Is Gretzky guilty? All of a sudden, Gretzky couldn't be trusted. If he was involved in the gambling ring, maybe he wasn't infallible—maybe he made mistakes in selecting players for Team Canada. Of course, anything to do with Canadian hockey will always be scrutinized with a fine-toothed comb, but this became the story, and as Canada drifted through the preliminary round with lackluster performance after lackluster performance, it was hard not to wonder whether Canada would have been better off without the Great One.

As for "Alexander the Great," while Canada was drifting through the round robin, he was busy sparking his Russian team. In eight games, Ovechkin scored five goals, including the game winner against the Canadians in the Olympic quarterfinal. Once again, Canada looked listless throughout their do-or-die matchup against Team Russia. Although they set a physical tone by banging the Russians around, they never really intimidated the Russians. Unlike the 2002 Olympics in which Paul Kariya and Mario Lemieux gave Canada an offensive flare to go along with their physical strength, the body checking felt empty throughout the 2006 Olympics.

Sure enough, after carrying the bulk of the play and looking more dangerous when they produced chances, Russia finally opened the scoring early in the third period. Ovechkin, who'd been circling through the slot like a hungry vulture, finally cruised towards the net, took a pass and one-timed the puck over Martin Brodeur's right shoulder. As is often the case in games that go scoreless for a long time, this opening goal stood up as the winner. Russia added a second, but Ovechkin's goal finished the comatose Canadians.

Unfortunately for Ovechkin and his Russian teammates, after knocking their archrivals out of the Olympics, they couldn't carry the momentum through to their semifinal matchup against Finland. After losing 4–0 to the Finns, Russia then lost their bronze-medal match against the Czech Republic 3–0.

The 2006–07 Season

After his sensational rookie season, Ovechkin and the Washington Capitals had dreams of making the playoffs. In Ovechkin's first year, Washington had been competitive but managed only 29 wins and 70 points. Unfortunately, neither the Capitals nor Ovechkin progressed very much in 2006–07. By no means did Ovechkin suffer from the sophomore jinx. Although his numbers dipped slightly in his second season as he failed to crack the 50-goal and 100-point barriers (82-46-46-92), it was another strong season in which Ovechkin proved that he was a consistent threat who had no trouble dealing with the relentless media attention.

Naturally, fame and attention brought greater expectations. In the District Capital, fans were hoping that Ovechkin's personal success would translate into team success. But 2006–07 was another mediocre season for the Washington Capitals, as they flirted with playoff contention, only to fall well short in the end. By duplicating their 70-point season of the previous year, the Caps again finished last in the weak Southeast Division. As for Ovechkin, despite posting solid offensive numbers, his defensive-zone coverage became a lightning rod for critics, pundits and fans. Questions began to surface about whether someone as goal-oriented as Ovechkin could lead any team to the promised land. Concerns about his "Russian-ness" also made some waves in the rumor mill—on call-in shows and in online forums, people wondered whether Ovechkin could prove himself a leader capable of elevating the play of his teammates.

In hindsight, the team was more inexperienced than bad, and both Ovechkin and the Caps needed to deal with some healthy adversity. The challenge going forward was for Washington to improve its team defense and for Ovechkin to develop into a defensive force rather than remaining a liability. Although Washington's team defense in 2006–07 was porous in general, Ovechkin led the way by posting a team-worst plus-minus of –19, a dubious stat for a player who scores 46 goals. Given the disparity between his offensive and defensive numbers, it was easy to read Ovechkin's game as one-dimensional. Since his sophomore season, Ovechkin has addressed his defensive short-comings. In both 2007–08 and 2008–09, he led his team to the playoffs and won the Hart Trophy as the NHL MVP.

The 2007–08 Season

On the heels of an up-and-down season in which Washington failed to turn the corner and make the playoffs, the 2007–08 season proved to the hockey world that Ovechkin had now evolved into a dominant two-way player. From the beginning of the season, his singular focus was making the playoffs.

"I'm hungry for hockey," Ovechkin said during training camp. "I can't wait until the season starts. We have a stronger team right now. I can feel it in the locker room. This atmosphere…everyone is happier, everyone is hungry."

At only 22 years of age, Ovechkin spent the season proving to everyone that he was now the best player in the world. He scored 65 goals, which marked the first time a player had hit the 60-goal mark since 1995–96, when both Mario Lemieux and Jaromir Jagr accomplished the feat. Ovechkin also led the NHL in points with 112 (82-65-47-112). At the end of the year, Ovechkin took home four trophies. For leading the league in goals, he won the Rocket Richard Trophy; for scoring the most points, he won the Art Ross Trophy; for being the MVP as voted by NHL players, he won the Lester B. Pearson Trophy; and for being the MVP as voted by members of the Professional Hockey Writers' Association, he won the Hart Memorial Trophy.

After a season in which observers had wondered how much of a team player Ovechkin would prove to be, he answered his critics by playing solid defense and by taking another step forward in his offensive evolution. "I'm the happiest 22-year-old guy on the planet," Ovechkin told reporters while posing for photos with four glittering pieces of hardware in front of him. "Everything I have got, I make myself. I'm working hard, and I know it's improving. I want to win everything. So next year, maybe the Stanley Cup."

The Russian Evolution

During Ovechkin's rookie season, *Sports Illustrated*'s pre-eminent hockey writer Michael Farber wrote a compelling article about Ovechkin called "The Russian Evolution." The article explored the ways in which Ovechkin represents a new breed of Russian hockey player who may be capable of not only winning a championship but also carrying his team to a championship the way Gretzky, Lemieux and Messier once did for their teams. As Farber points out, in the brief history of Russians playing in the NHL, few have been the key component on championship teams. Moreover, none of the biggest Russian stars have carried a franchise to a Stanley Cup championship. Ovechkin, however, may change that landscape. In Farber's words, "If no Russian has been able to carry his team to a title, well, no Russian plays quite like Ovechkin, a right-handed shooting left wing who combines great speed, dazzling creativity and a willingness to go through defensemen as well as around them. He is the Russian Evolution."

One exception to Farber's theory may be Sergei Fedorov, who won three Stanley Cups in Detroit and played a crucial role in each of the Red Wings' runs. But skeptics could argue that Detroit was Steve Yzerman's team during the first two Cup runs—and those skeptics would, of course, be right. The other glaring exception is Evgeni Malkin, who became the first Russian to win the Conn Smythe Trophy as the playoff MVP (2009). Although Sidney Crosby tends to get the lion's share of the press, Malkin has quietly benefited from playing second fiddle to Crosby, and he is now emerging as a more lethal offensive player. Still, Pittsburgh seems to be Crosby's team. And, besides, like Ovechkin, Malkin is part of the Russian Evolution.

Now four years into his career, Ovechkin is proving that he is a team player who is the engine behind Washington's success. As he goes, so go the Caps. During the 2007–08 season, Ovechkin's nightly heroics helped put Washington back into the playoffs. As impressive as his offensive numbers were, it was his defensive play that helped Washington become a better team. A year after posting a team-worst plus-minus rating of −19, Ovechkin addressed his defensive-zone issues and posted an impressive +28. All of a sudden, Ovechkin was seeing ice time at the end of games when Washington had a lead to defend. Collectively, the Caps had become a solid defensive team, and they hadn't sacrificed any offense to get there. The impact on their bottom line was remarkable. A year after finishing 14th out of 15 teams in the Eastern Conference,

Washington won the Southeast Division in 2007–08 and finished third in the conference.

There were, of course, many reasons for the team's dramatic turnaround, but one of the most underrated factors was "belief." With Ovechkin, Washington was now playing like a team that believed anything was possible. As defenseman Shaone Morrisonn summed it up, "He believes, so we believe." As a statement of Ovechkin's impact on the team, it's simple yet profound. In hockey, believing is half the battle, and when a team features the intimidating presence of a man like Ovechkin who scores big goals at crucial times and steamrolls people for the fun of it, wouldn't you believe?

Two other noteworthy factors were part of Washington's return to the playoffs. The first was the continued development of a strong core of young players. Alongside Ovechkin, Washington featured a plethora of supremely talented players. During their rebuilding years in the early 2000s, Washington had managed to stockpile draft picks, often adding a pick somewhere in the first round to go along with their own. Between 2002 and 2008, the Capitals drafted 14 players in the first round, including Alexander Ovechkin, Mike Green, Alexander Semin, Nicklas Backstrom, Jeff Schultz, Simeon Varlamov and the emerging defenseman Karl Alzner. During the 2007–08 season, Green, Backstrom and Semin emerged as a viable supporting cast for Alexander the Great. In addition, Washington GM George McPhee made a couple of small moves at the trading deadline to add some experience to his young nucleus. Most significantly, Sergei Fedorov was brought in to bolster the center-ice position, to add a veteran Russian presence, to play a leadership role on the team and to serve as a mentor for Ovechkin and Semin.

The second factor in Washington's turnaround was a well-timed coaching change. Since Ovechkin had entered the league, Glen Hanlon had been behind the Washington bench. After a poor start to the 2007–08 season (Washington came out of the gates with a 6-14-1 record), Hanlon was replaced by Bruce Boudreau, a career minor-league coach who had loads of coaching experience but none at the NHL level. But things shifted on a dime in Washington as soon as Boudreau took over the reins. En route to winning the Jack Adams Trophy as the NHL Coach of the Year, Boudreau compiled a 37-17-7 record over the balance of the season.

Unfortunately, Washington's regular-season success didn't translate into playoff success. In the opening round, Washington faced the Philadelphia

Flyers and lost a hard-fought series in heart-breaking fashion. By virtue of having won their division, Washington had home-ice advantage, but they fell behind in the series three games to one, only to come storming back. After winning game five at home, Washington went on the road and managed to beat Philly on their own rink, and Ovechkin made the difference.

Despite an inconsistent series, Ovechkin showed up in game six at just the right time. Down 3–2 in the series and facing elimination for the second straight game, Washington dropped behind 2–0 early in the game. But after Alexander Semin and Nicklas Backstrom changed the momentum with second-period goals, Ovechkin took over in the third. Two minutes into the final frame, after a sloppy turn-over by the Flyers at the offensive blue line, Ovechkin split the defense and took a long stretch pass from Viktor Kozlov. Alone from the red line in, Ovechkin roared in on goal, deked Martin Biron to his knees and then buried the puck upstairs. It was a crucial go-ahead goal early in the third, and Washington never looked back. Halfway through the period, Ovechkin put the icing on the cake with a one-timer on the power play.

The victory forced a decisive seventh game, and with the series heading back to the Verizon

Center in Washington, the Caps had all the momentum on their side. In the opening minute of the game, Ovechkin set the tone by nailing Kimmo Timonen behind the Philadelphia net. A few minutes later, Washington capitalized on a two-man advantage to claim the early lead. Ovechkin had hammered the puck just wide, but the ricochet came off the boards and onto Nicklas Backstrom's stick, and he buried the biscuit.

But Philly proved a resilient bunch, and they answered right back. On a power play of their own, Scottie Upshall scored. Then, halfway through the second, Sami Kapanen put the Flyers ahead. But just as the Flyers appeared to be taking control of the game, Ovechkin stepped up and put Washington back on even terms with a heavy wrist shot that he blew by Flyers' goalie Martin Biron. After a scoreless third period, game seven went into sudden-death overtime.

Five minutes into the extra frame, Washington's Tom Poti took a chintzy tripping penalty to put his team short-handed. After peppering the Caps' Cristobal Huet during the man advantage, Joffrey Lupul picked up a rebound and managed to slide the puck past Huet's outstretched leg. Just like that, Washington was finished.

Despite the disappointing first-round loss, Washington had plenty of cause for optimism.

They were, after all, an extremely young team with 15 players who had been playoff rookies going into the series against Philadelphia. In addition to the countless awards and achievements Ovechkin's stellar season had earned him, the Capitals franchise was clearly back on the NHL map, as seen by a statement made on the team's Facebook page:

> *It's been a long time, but the tide has turned both on and off the ice for the Washington Capitals. For the first time in five years, the Caps are back in the Stanley Cup playoffs. With one of the youngest teams in the league, some of the league's most exciting young players and a bevy of young and talented players still rising through the ranks, the future—both immediate and long term—looks very bright for the Capitals.*

The 2008–09 Season

Brimming with exuberance, confidence and optimism, Ovechkin entered the 2008–09 season and repeated as the league MVP. His numbers, though down slightly, were still among the best in the league. For the second straight year, he won the Rocket Richard Trophy as the NHL's leading goal scorer with 56 goals (79-56-54-110). As a team, Washington took a few more strides. One year older and a year wiser, Ovechkin's supporting cast was also better. In particular, the slick-passing centerman Nicklas Backstrom, the smooth-skating defenseman Mike Green and the other Russian sniper Alexander Semin proved themselves to be world-class players. Washington improved their point total by 14 points. With 50 wins and 108 points, the Capitals finished second in the Eastern Conference behind only the New Jersey Devils.

In terms of the media attention on Ovechkin, it became clear during the 2008–09 season that the young Russian was now the kingpin of the league. Of course, this is not to take anything away from the stellar play of Sidney Crosby and Evgeni Malkin, but Ovechkin's personality resonates at a rare frequency. An emotional person who wears his heart on his sleeve and doesn't rely on clichés to communicate, it is difficult not to respect, admire and cheer for Ovechkin. Unless, of course, you happen to be Don Cherry and your patriotic myopia won't allow you to love anything beyond the emblematic Canadian hockey player who brings his lunch pail every night, grinds in the corners like groundhog and contributes little to the end result beyond the overrated quality of passion.

For the sake of recapping the harmless war of words that took place during the 2008–09 season between Ovechkin and Cherry—two of hockey's most colorful characters—Ovechkin started it by celebrating his goals in a way that drove Cherry bananas. Long before Ovechkin's notorious 50-goal celebration, he had no doubt irked Cherry and other hockey purists during the NHL All-Star Game, when he somehow managed to breathe some life into hockey's annual snoozefest by adding a little theater to the drab spectacle.

In the previous year's 2008 NHL All-Star Game, Ovechkin earned the loudest cheers during the skills competition by juggling the puck on the blade of his stick during the breakaway challenge. After tapping the puck several times, he sent it 20 feet into the air, executed a spin-o-rama and then took a baseball swing at the disc. He missed, but the crowd ate it up. For the 2008–09 All-Star Game in Montréal, Ovechkin had something even more adventurous up his sleeve.

Playing up the rumored friction between himself and Malkin, Ovechkin entered the final round of the breakaway challenge and used Malkin as his buddy. Given 60 seconds to play around on breakaway after breakaway, midway through his allotted time, Ovechkin skated over to Malkin, who provided the props. First, Malkin handed

Ovechkin an Australian bush hat with a mini Canadian flag sticking out of it; Ovechkin then put on a pair of flashy sunglasses, which Malkin quickly polished with a shammy; then came a quick squirt of Gatorade and a second stick. The shtick was now in full swing. Ovechkin came across the blue line batting the puck back and forth between the two sticks. He then tossed one of the sticks aside and fired the puck on net with the other. It was saved, but like a good goal scorer, he stayed with the play and banged in the rebound. The crowd went nuts, laughing along with Ovechkin and cheering his willingness to have fun and play the clown.

When people criticize such antics, it is hard to imagine where they're coming from. In all likelihood, it is nothing more than good old-fashioned jealousy—or maybe the problem is that Ovechkin is branded as a show-off, which of course he is. But hockey is an emotional and a physical game in which the fans play a vital role in the success of the sport. Ovechkin contributes to the spectacle, and his enthusiasm is contagious. In other words, he loves life, and when people see that, they feed off it. But Ovechkin is by no means conventional, and so he challenges the status quo, which is intimidating for anyone who has a fixed idea of what hockey should be and where the boundaries lie between sport and spectacle.

In any case, Ovechkin's unique qualities as a human being are what make him a great hockey player and a compelling athlete. His charisma and energy are also the reason he now seems to be moving beyond the cloistered world of hockey and into the North American mainstream. The reason for his public success is that, instead of giving us the same old thing, Ovechkin always surprises. When he plays, he has the enthusiasm of a boy playing a game. And when he scores, his excitement is released in a frantic celebration. Like his hockey game, Ovechkin also boasts an impressive variety of celebrations. One of his best moves—which he seems to pull out only for truly thrilling goals, such as game winners or unbelievable individual efforts—is an adapted variation of the Lambeau Leap. After scoring, Ovechkin will skate full speed towards the boards and leap into the glass, as if delivering a body check. The crowd, of course, goes mental.

Ever the innovator, when Ovechkin scored his 50th goal in the 2008–09 season, he brought out some new material. Headed for the goal, he came down the right wing and snapped a wicked wrist shot to the far corner over the goalie's glove. As the goal went in, Ovechkin's momentum took him behind the Tampa net, where he threw on the brakes, dropped his stick to the ice and held his hands over the stick as if it were on fire and too hot to pick up. As defenseman Mike Green entered the picture to congratulate his teammate, Ovechkin motioned for Green to stay back, that he shouldn't get near the burning stick.

After these innocent shenanigans, the media managed to stir up an odd uproar about whether the charade was in poor taste. The goal was scored against the bottom-feeding Tampa Bay Lightning, whose season had been a disaster from day one. Was it necessary to rub salt into Tampa's wounds by gloating after a goal? From the antiquated perspective of a man like Don Cherry, it was most definitely in bad taste.

The irony is that despite his own flamboyance, Cherry doesn't seem to endorse any on-ice theatrics other than fighting. Of course, part of the problem Cherry has with Ovechkin is that he isn't Canadian, and although Cherry will occasionally acknowledge that Ovechkin is supremely talented, he just can't bring himself to offer any sincere compliments to the game's best player.

Although Cherry gave Ovechkin a pretty stern lecture on "Coach's Corner" after Ovechkin's 50th-goal celebration (the basic lesson was that taunting a downtrodden team is a hockey faux pas), Cherry has also compared Ovechkin to soccer players who celebrate goals by dancing or doing back flips. It was as if we must all agree that watching a Brazilian football player score a majestic goal and then celebrate it by dancing the cha-cha-cha is a stain upon the game. On this occasion, Cherry's rant toed the line between patriotism and payback:

> *What I try to do is teach the kids the Canadian way. What we have to watch is we don't start acting like those goofy soccer guys.... Kids—Act like Joe Thornton, act like Joe Sakic, act like Iginla, Shanahan, Bobby Orr, Yzerman.... Look at this guy* [Ovechkin], *you know what, I'm gonna tell you about this guy.... He runs at guys, does this stuff.... There's somebody out there, some big defenseman is gonna be sittin' in the weeds as he cuts across center ice, somebody's gonna cut him in half. You don't act like this goof.*

Aside from lecturing Canadian kids about proper hockey etiquette, Cherry's trip into fantasyland is especially revealing. By imagining a Scott Stevens prototype on a revenge-seeking mission, Cherry is more or less invoking The Code, that unwritten book of regulations that players abide by in order to defend each other and each other's honor. In Ovechkin's case, Cherry is suggesting that Ovechkin will pay for insulting his opponent's honor by taunting them. But Ovechkin doesn't seem to mind. After Cherry chimed in with his two cents, Ovechkin was asked what he thought of Cherry's reaction.

"Different minds," Ovechkin began with a shrug. "Old people—they don't like when people show some energy, some emotions. So they're like robots." At this point, Ovechkin broke into a pretty good robot dance. "You. Can't. Go. Like. This," he continued, simulating a robotic monotone. "You. Have. To. Skate. Like. This. Uh. Uh. Uh. Don't. Celebration. When. You. Score. Goals. Thank. You. Don." End scene.

The 2009 Playoffs

The 2008–09 regular season was one of the most successful seasons in franchise history for the Washington Capitals. But after losing a thrilling seven-game series to the Philadelphia Flyers in 2007–08, the Capitals were looking to follow up their stellar regular season by moving deep into the NHL playoffs. In the opening round, Washington was matched up against the New York Rangers, a stingy defensive team with a few dangerous offensive weapons—Chris Drury, Scott Gomez and Markus Naslund—who had underperformed during the regular season.

For the second year in a row, Washington got off to a terrible start in the playoffs. In the first game, they played well and controlled the tempo of the game, but lost 4–3. Starting goaltender José Théodore, who had been signed to a big free-agent contract in the off-season, had a poor game. Although there hadn't been any major gaffes, the storyline after game one was that Henrik Lundqvist had stood on his head for New York, while Washington didn't get timely saves from their keeper.

Had it been a rare off night, coach Bruce Boudreau might have stuck with Théodore. But Washington had gotten inconsistent goal-tending from Théodore throughout the year, and Boudreau decided to take a risk by starting rookie Russian netminder Simeon Varlamov in game two. Washington lost the game, but the score was 1–0 and Varlamov was scintillating in the Washington net.

Down 2–0 after their two home games, Washington went to Madison Square Garden (MSG) and managed to split the two games. They came home for game five in the same hole they had dug for themselves the previous year against the Flyers. The Caps needed three straight wins, which is always a tall order in the heightened intensity of playoff atmosphere. Fortunately for Washington, New York didn't bother showing up for game five, and the Caps cruised to a 4–0 win. Varlamov was now turning into a major subplot. He gave the Caps solid goaltending, and, despite limited NHL experience, the young Russian didn't seem to mind the playoff spotlight.

Game six was back in New York at MSG, and once again the Rangers played a lackluster game. The Caps jumped out to a 3–1 lead after one, and they extended their lead to 5–1 before New York added a couple of late markers to make the final 5–3.

The decisive seventh game was a goaltender's duel. The teams traded first-period goals and then the game settled into a defensive battle. Throughout the game, Washington had the lion's share of the quality scoring chances, and they finally capitalized on one of them late in the third period. Sergei Fedorov, the 39-year-old three-time Stanley Cup champion, skated over the Ranger blue line on his off wing. Using Ovechkin as a decoy, Fedorov stopped at the faceoff dot and snapped a shot into the top corner of the net over Lundqvist's left shoulder. Washington won the game 2–1 and the series 4–3.

Alexander the Great vs. Sid the Kid

Going into the second round, a plethora of compelling storylines circulated through the media, but everything was overshadowed by the Ovechkin-Crosby rivalry. Since their rookie seasons, Ovechkin and Crosby have been the two most marketable commodities in the NHL. They have both lived up to their hype and helped the NHL overcome its PR problem after the lockout. The rivalry between the two megastars had been brewing for four years, but with their teams facing each other in a seven-game series, the world would finally get to see Ovechkin and Crosby go head-to-head for all the marbles.

Besides the Ovechkin-Crosby rivalry, one of the central questions going into the second round revolved around Washington's 21-year-old rookie goaltender, the acrobatic Simeon Varlamov. During the regular season, Varlamov had played sparingly. In six games, he had played well, posting a 4-0-1 record with a 2.37 goals-against average and a 0.918 save percentage. But six regular-season games is nothing to go by. And even though he had played well in relief for José Théodore in the opening round, everyone wondered whether Varlamov would buckle under the burden of expectation.

In the series opener, Varlamov answered his doubters with a Tretiak-like 34-save performance that helped Washington take the game 3–2. Despite letting in a pair of questionable goals, Varlamov also made a few miraculous saves when his team needed them. If one thing was clear from game one, it was that both teams were content playing a thrilling back-and-forth style of hockey reminiscent of the wide-open 1980s.

Game two will go down as one of the greatest showdowns in hockey history. The series had been billed as Ovechkin vs. Crosby, and the second game brought the rivalry to life. Crosby opened the scoring by banging in a goalmouth pass on a first-period power play. In the second period, Ovechkin answered Crosby's goal by ripping a wicked one-timer past a sprawling Marc-André Fleury.

Not to be outdone, Crosby restored Pittsburgh's lead halfway through the second by fishing a loose puck out of Varlamov's crease and tapping it in. Prior to the second intermission, David Steckel put Washington back on even terms by finding a rebound in front of Fleury and roofing it home. The Steckel goal set the stage for a scintillating third period in which Ovechkin and Crosby stepped up and delivered prime-time performances.

In the third period, with the score still tied at two, Washington continued their dominance by cleanly winning an offensive zone faceoff. As the puck came back to Mike Green at the right point, Ovechkin backpedaled from the top of the faceoff circle to the right point. Green played a soft pass into his wheelhouse, and Ovechkin unleashed a cannon that Fleury couldn't handle. The goal put Washington into the lead. Ovechkin went nuts and leaped into the Plexiglas before his teammates mobbed him.

But Ovechkin wasn't done. Less than three minutes later, he took a pass at center and stepped into the offensive zone with a defenseman in front of him. Using the defenseman as a screen, Ovechkin wired a quick wrist shot past Fleury, who seemed surprised by the shot. As hats came raining down onto the Verizon Center ice in recognition of Ovechkin's hat trick, the scene was bedlam. In the game's final minute, as Pittsburgh desperately tried to mount a comeback, Crosby managed to bang in his third goal of the evening, and although the Penguins came up short, the matching hat tricks were a fitting result for the league's marquee superstars, who had gone head-to-head and met each other punch-for-punch.

With Washington up 2–0 and in the driver's seat, the scene shifted to Pittsburgh for games three and four. Game three was another tightly contested affair that started disastrously for Pittsburgh as Fleury came out of his net to play the puck only to drop his stick. In a terrible stroke of bad luck for the Penguins, the puck then ricocheted off Fleury's discarded stick and directly into the slot. And guess who was cruising through the slot ready to pounce on Pittsburgh's misfortune? Ovechkin swooped in and one-timed the puck into the open net while Fleury scrambled in vain to get back to his net. The goal came in the second minute of play.

From that point on, however, Pittsburgh played a strong game. One of the difference makers in this third game was Evgeni Malkin, who had been oddly quiet in the first two games. He scored Pittsburgh's go-ahead goal, and even though Nicklas Backstrom sent the game into overtime with a late third-period tally, Kris Letang scored the overtime winner on a harmless-looking slap shot from the point that somehow eluded Simeon Varlamov.

In game four, there seemed to be a chink in Varlamov's armor. Although he continued to make some spectacular saves, he gave up a couple more weak goals that helped Pittsburgh build a 3–1 lead after the first period. Washington proved to be resilient in coming back, but they could never quite make up the gap, and the game ended 5–3. Game five went back to Washington with the series leveled at two.

After a scoreless first period, the floodgates opened after Jordan Staal scored for the Penguins five minutes into the second period. Ovechkin, who has a knack of scoring timely goals, tied the game less than a minute later. In the third period, with Pittsburgh now leading 3–2, Ovechkin came through in the clutch. With less than five minutes to play, on a beautiful three-way passing play, Green found Backstrom in the slot, who then fed the puck to Ovechkin on the right wing, and Ovechkin fired the puck home. For the second time in the series, the game went into overtime, and this time, Evgeni Malkin provided the heroics. Three minutes into the extra frame, Malkin scored a fluke goal that caromed past Varlamov off Tom Poti's outstretched stick.

As the series returned to Pittsburgh, it was now becoming clear that this second-round series would prove to be the highlight of the 2009 playoffs. Through five games, the pace had been frantic, the goaltending acrobatic, the stars were rising to the occasion, and none of the games had been blowouts. With Washington now facing elimination, the game was once again fast paced and full of scoring chances. After three periods, the game was tied 4–4. For the third time in the series, overtime was needed. This time, though, Washington came out on top as David Steckel scored the sudden-death winner by deflecting in a point shot.

Unfortunately, after an amazing series that featured some of the most exciting hockey in the past decade, Pittsburgh ran away with game seven. After Marc-André Fleury made a glorious save on an early Ovechkin breakaway, the Penguins took control of the game by scoring two goals eight seconds apart in the first period.

In the second period, Pittsburgh added three more, to take a 5–0 lead. Although Ovechkin came back with his 11th goal in his 14th playoff game (14-11-10-21), the Capitals were facing too large a deficit. The game ended 6–2, and Washington was sent packing while Pittsburgh continued on their Stanley Cup run.

After sweeping the Carolina Hurricanes in four games to earn the Eastern Conference berth, the Penguins exacted some revenge upon the defending Stanley Cup champions. In a well-played seven-game final, Pittsburgh came out on top to claim their first Stanley Cup since 1992, when Mario Lemieux led the Penguins to their second straight title. Evgeni Malkin was named the Conn Smythe winner and Sidney Crosby, the 21-year-old captain of the Penguins, got to raise the Stanley Cup. The whole scene must have turned Ovechkin's stomach.

Chapter Four

The Soviet Invasion

The Dawn of Russian Hockey

Compared to Canada or the U.S., Russia is a young hockey nation. In the 1920s and 1930s, Russians played an ice sport called "bandy"; it was more or less a soccer-hockey hybrid. Although played on ice, the game took place on large frozen fields that were more like soccer fields than hockey rinks, being both bigger and without boards. Also like soccer, the game was played with 11 players per side, and it emphasized speed, skill and ball possession.

At this time in Canada, on the other hand, hockey was already firmly established as an important cultural activity. Although hockey's history in Canada is somewhat debatable, the first organized indoor game took place on March 5, 1875, at the Victoria Skating Rink in Montréal. Of course, prior to this level of organization, games of shinny had been common since roughly the turn of the 19th century. In Scandinavia, that other great hockey hotbed, hockey's roots go back to a form of bandy similar to the Russian game but with large, soccer-sized nets.

The Russian version, in contrast, used smaller nets, which, of course, made it harder to score. Because of the hockey-sized nets, the Russian style of bandy emphasized precise shooting and long buildups. As such, it was a possession game. Goals were often the result of several precise passes that allowed the attacking team to penetrate the opposition's defense and move in tight on the small net.

In the Soviet Union, the shift from bandy to hockey was likely catalyzed by the visit of a team of players from the German Labour Sport Union, which visited Moscow in 1932 to demonstrate the Canadian game of hockey. Although the series of hockey games played between Russian bandy players and the Germans had little immediate impact, it was noted by *Spartak* (a Leningrad-based newspaper) that because ice hockey required less space, it was easier to prepare the field for a game. At that time, plowing snow from the surface was extremely laborious, a fact that helped hockey gain traction on Russian soil.

By 1938, the first hockey rink was built in the eastern section of Dynamo's stadium in Moscow. Dynamo, as stated earlier, is a Moscow-based sports club that consists of several professional organizations, including hockey, soccer, basketball and even bandy. As a result of the hybrid nature of bandy, many of the early Soviet hockey stars were also soccer and bandy players. Vsevolod Bobrov, for example, was a soccer star prior to becoming a Russian hockey star.

It was during this post-war period that Russian hockey really took off, and it should surprise no one that the reasons for its growth were largely political. A major landmark occurred in March 1948 when LTC Prague, the best European hockey team at the time, came to Moscow for a tournament against a team of Soviet stars. The event was a huge success for Soviet hockey because the games attracted crowds of over 30,000 people and the Soviet team was very competitive; they won the first game 6–3, lost the second 5–3 and tied the third. This event, along with the general development of the game throughout the Soviet Union, caused Joseph Stalin to realize the global impact Russian hockey could have as the battle over political ideologies known as the Cold War continued into the 1950s.

Although Russians were still better bandy players than they were hockey players, Stalin realized that bandy had virtually no international interest, whereas hockey now had a yearly international competition called the World Championships, and it was also a recognized Olympic sport. Having now seen that Russia could compete against a team of Czech stars, Stalin began to understand that hockey could play a role in promoting communism to the rest of the international community. From this point forward, hockey was supported in the Soviet Union at the highest political level, which meant money for building a hockey infrastructure and developing players who could eventually compete with and defeat the vaunted Canadians.

But before going international, Stalin and his Kremlin cohorts wanted to be certain they could win. Phase one of the plan to achieve global hockey dominance was for Anatoly Tarasov to develop the Russian style. Tarasov, who is now widely regarded as the grandfather of Russian hockey, was a player-coach for CSKA Moscow, a team run by the Soviet Red Army.

Once the political decision had been made to become dominant on the international scene, Tarasov was put in charge of defining what Russian hockey would be. Initially, he wanted to visit Canada for inspiration on hockey greatness, but his mentor Mikhail Tavarovsky refused. "There's nothing for you in Canada," Tavarovsky said. "Devise your own style."

And so that's precisely what Tarasov did. Instead of copying the Canadian brand of hockey, Tarasov adapted the skills that Soviet players had developed over years of playing bandy to a hockey rink: fast skating, crisp passing and pin-point shooting accuracy. Tarasov's motto was "Don't shoot unless you're certain to score."

Of course, because of the government and military involvement at the time, the most talented Soviet athletes to emerge in the following decades lived and breathed hockey. Often housed in barracks with limited access to their families (if they managed to have one), the best Soviet stars inevitably played for CSKA Moscow. More commonly referred to in the West as the Red Army because of its affiliation with the Soviet military, the club was formed in 1946 and won 32 Soviet regular-season championships during the Soviet League's 46-year history. The reason for the club's dominance had to do with the country's mandatory military service. Because of the army's involvement in the club, CSKA would just draft the best players into the army, and hockey served as their military duty. Furthermore, because all of the best players played for the Red Army, the national team was basically the same team, only the national team wore CCCP (the Russian initials for the Union of Soviet Socialist Republics, or more commonly, the USSR) on their jerseys instead of CSKA.

By the time the 1980s rolled around, a few Soviet players—most notably Igor Larionov and Viacheslav Fetisov—had started speaking out about their desire to play in the NHL. In particular, Larionov had been imagining the possibility of playing NHL hockey since the 1981 Canada Cup when he first visited Canadian soil. As the decade wore on, the Soviet Union started a slow shift away from communism. The transition towards open markets and greater freedom of speech and information began around 1985, when Mikhail Gorbachev came to power. In particular, Gorbachev's glasnost (**Гласность**) policy was designed to increase the openness and transparency of all government institutions by reducing corruption in the upper echelons of the Communist Party and the Soviet government. This policy also began the slow process of decreasing censorship while facilitating greater freedom of information.

Within a few years, the social reality in the Soviet Union had changed enough for a few hockey players to negotiate NHL contracts. In most cases, a portion of the player's salary went to his Soviet club as compensation for the loss of their resource. On March 31, 1989, Sergei Priakin became the first Russian to play an NHL game; he had been drafted by the Calgary Flames as the last overall pick in 1988. Although Priakin is little more than a historical footnote, the event signaled a massive change for the NHL. As the first player to gain permission from the Soviet Ice Hockey Federation to play in the NHL, Priakin opened the floodgates for the so-called Russian Invasion. Soon after Priakin came to North America, the Federation was reformed, and the changes made it much easier for Russian players to sign with the NHL teams that held their rights.

The following season, 10 Russian players were in training camps across the NHL vying for spots. Unlike Priakin, a mediocre right winger who was a fringe player for the Flames, many of the players who debuted in the fall of 1989 were already legends in the Soviet Union, having cemented their greatness as teammates with the Red Army (CSKA Moscow) and the national team (CCCP). These stars included defenseman Viacheslav Fetisov (who started his NHL career with the New Jersey Devils) and the three members of the famed KLM line—Vladimir Krutov, Igor Larionov and Sergei Makarov. Both Larionov and Krutov debuted for the Vancouver Canucks, while Makarov joined the Calgary Flames.

Although Larionov and Fetisov went on to have long NHL careers, it was Makarov who had the most dramatic impact in his first NHL season. He won the Calder Trophy as the NHL's Rookie of the Year, even though he was 31 years old and a nine-time Soviet scoring champion. The NHL amended its eligibility rules the following year by adding the "Makarov Rule," which stipulates that players must be under the age of 26 to qualify for the award.

Given this historical backdrop, and the fact that Canadians had relatively little exposure to these Soviet-era stars other than in the Summit Series of 1972 and the Canada Cups of 1976, 1981, 1984 and 1987, let us take a look back at the 10 greatest Soviet hockey stars.

Top 10 Soviet Greats

10. Boris Mikhailov

Famous for wearing the dreaded number 13, Boris Mikhailov played a decidedly Canadian role on one of hockey's greatest lines. Alongside the slickness and speed of linemates Valeri Kharlamov and Vladimir Petrov, Boris Mikhailov was a grinder and a mucker who won loose pucks, went to the net and wasn't afraid to get a little dirty if circumstances called for it.

In hockey's cold war—the 1972 Summit Series between Canada and the Soviet Union—Mikhailov was the guy who infamously kicked Gary Bergman, lacerating the Canadian defenseman's calf.

Despite the notorious gesture (which was returned in kind by Bobby Clarke when he gave Valeri Kharlamov a wicked two-handed slash to the ankle), Mikhailov was a tremendous hockey player who had a knack for being opportunistic and scoring big goals. In World and Olympic Championships combined, Mikhailov played in 120 games, scoring 108 goals and 77 assists. He led the Soviet League in scoring three times and was twice named its MVP.

9. Vladimir Krutov

Despite being unceremoniously dubbed "Vladimir Crouton" and "Vlad the Inhaler" during his underwhelming stint in the NHL as a Vancouver Canuck, Krutov was a machine in the Soviet League and in international play. More favorably known as "The Tank" in the Soviet Union, Krutov was built like a brick outhouse and had soft goal-scorer's hands. Internationally, he was a member of the Soviet national teams that won, among other things, the 1981 Canada Cup, two Olympic gold medals and six World Championships. But in all likelihood, Canadians will remember his superlative play at the 1987 Canada Cup. Along with Wayne Gretzky and Mario Lemieux, Krutov was named a tournament all-star after recording seven goals and eight assists for 15 points. Along with stalwart defenseman Viacheslav Fetisov, Krutov was the Soviet Union's most dominant player.

Unfortunately, once he hit the NHL, the lure of Western freedom seemed to be the death of him. After showing up for training camp in Vancouver overweight and out of shape, Krutov added to his problem with some questionable dietary habits. According to former Canucks' coach Bob McCammon, "His usual routine was to stop at a 7-Eleven store and order two hot dogs, a bag of potato chips and a soft drink. After practice, he would return for a second order." Following a mediocre year in Vancouver in which he showed flashes of brilliance and a lot of bad defensive habits, Krutov finished his playing career in Switzerland and Sweden.

8. Anatoly Firsov

One of only four players to have his number retired in Soviet hockey (Bobrov, Tretiak and Kharlamov are the others), Anatoly Firsov was the original Russian Rocket. But Firsov was also a tremendously creative player with a Gretzky-like imagination. Unfortunately, in the buildup to the 1972 Summit Series, the Soviet national team was undergoing an internal power struggle between long-time coach Anatoly Tarasov and the heir apparent Vsevolod Bobrov. Bobrov wound up winning the battle to coach the Soviets against Team Canada, and Firsov's loyalty to Tarasov resulted in his refusal to play. As a result, Canadian hockey fans were never really privy to his greatness.

7. Vsevolod Bobrov

After serving in the Soviet Army during World War II, Bobrov spent the next decade playing both hockey and soccer at the highest level. Like Bo Jackson and Deion Sanders in the modern sports era, Vsevolod Bobrov was in all likelihood the greatest two-sport athlete of the post-war period. The fact that he had also been a soldier only speaks to the tremendous physical prowess and athleticism Bobrov must have possessed.

In 1945, fresh off the heels of trench warfare, Bobrov led the Soviet Union's soccer league in goals with 24. That same year, he was invited to join Dynamo Moscow (Bobrov played for CSKA) as a guest player as they toured Europe to play some of the best clubs in European football—including Chelsea, Arsenal and Rangers. During the tour, Bobrov amazed everyone and scored six goals during the exhibition series. By the end of his soccer career (1945–53), Bobrov had won three Soviet Championships, having scored 97 goals in only 116 games, which is an astonishing clip for any era in soccer.

During his heyday as a soccer player, Bobrov was in fact an even better hockey player. You may recall that at Wayne Gretzky's peak, the Great One set the NHL goal-scoring record by potting 92 goals in only 80 games. In the process, he shattered the previous mark of 76 goals, which had been established by Phil Esposito in 1970–71. For the sake of comparison, Bobrov *averaged* nearly two goals per game. In only 130 games, he scored an amazing 254 goals while leading his team to seven Soviet Championships during a stellar 10-year career.

6. Igor Larionov

As the pivot for the legendary KLM line, Igor Larionov's greatest weapon was his intelligence. Often compared to Wayne Gretzky, Larionov may not have been quite the player Gretzky was, but he did possess similar passing skills and hockey sense. As for the chemistry he had with his two wingers, Vladimir Krutov and Sergei Makarov, Larionov summarized it this way:

> *Eight seasons we played together, side by side, day after day, and month after month. It was a tremendous chemistry between us and the way we played the game. We were able to showcase our game to rinks around the world. To me, that was a joy when you can create, paint a masterpiece,*

*and when you know that's going to hap-
pen every night you step on the ice. Fans
were excited to see us play and we enjoyed
playing for them and playing for the love
of the game.*

Along with Viacheslav Fetisov, Larionov was also instrumental in pushing to gain the right to leave the Soviet Union and sign NHL contracts. During his eight-year Soviet career, Larionov frequently went head-to-head with coach Viktor Tikhonov, who rarely allowed players to see their families. Instead of living at home, players spent as many as 11 months of the year in barracks, and their sole responsibility was to train and play hockey. Tikhonov, who coached Larionov both at the club level with CSKA Moscow and at the national level for CCCP, was a tremendous coach, but the strictness of his regime also pushed many of his players to fight fervently for greater freedom.

Finally, after years of lobbying, Larionov and a few other Soviet stars negotiated their release and in 1989, Fetisov, Makarov, Krutov and Larionov all joined the NHL. Although none of these Soviet legends proved to be veritable stars in the NHL, Larionov played a remarkable 15 years in the league. Dubbed "The Professor" because of his tremendous intelligence and high hockey IQ,

Larionov found his most effective role as a defensive specialist with the Detroit Red Wings.

During their heyday in the late '90s, the Red Wings often employed a five-man Russian unit that consisted of Larionov, Sergei Fedorov, Vyacheslav Kozlov, Viacheslav Fetisov and Vladimir Konstantinov. Together, the so-called Russian Five played a gorgeous, flowing style of hockey that combined speed, tape-to-tape passing and precision shooting. For Larionov, it must have felt like the old Soviet days, when part of the Soviet system was to consistently employ five-man units. For years, the KLM line played with Fetisov and Alexei Kasatonov. Collectively, they were known as the Green Unit. In 2008, Igor Larionov was inducted into the NHL Hall of Fame.

5. Sergei Makarov

Sergei Makarov had a glorious career as a sniper in the Soviet League. In his 11 seasons playing for CSKA Moscow, Makarov was the MVP of the league three times, and he won the Izvestia Trophy for leading the league in scoring an incredible nine times. Like his Soviet linemates Krutov and Larionov, Makarov joined the NHL in 1989.

As a playmaker, a scorer and a tremendous stickhandler, Makarov often found it frustrating playing the dump-and-chase hockey that is so often part of the North American game. Despite such issues, Makarov had a much better rookie season than his former linemates. After recording 24 goals and 62 assists for 86 points, Makarov won the Calder Trophy as the NHL Rookie of the Year.

4. Alexander Maltsev

As a kid growing up in Moscow, Alexander Ovechkin's favorite player was Alexander Maltsev, despite the fact that Maltsev retired the year before Ovechkin was born. Given Maltsev's legend in Moscow, though, it is not altogether surprising that a young hockey fanatic like Ovechkin would choose Maltsev as his man.

In the 1972 Summit Series, Maltsev was the setup man for Valeri Kharlamov, and the duo was as lethal as Gretzky and Lemieux were during the 1987 Canada Cup. Having said that, by the end of the Summit Series, when the Canadians were hitting everything they could see and the tenor of the series had reached its full pitch, Maltsev was less dominant.

Maltsev is also difficult to categorize because unlike nearly everyone else on this list, he didn't play for CSKA Moscow. Instead, Maltsev played for Moscow Dynamo, and during his illustrious career (1967–84), Maltsev led Dynamo to six silver medals and seven bronze medals. Unfortunately for him, because all the best players except for him played for CSKA, no other team really had a chance to win gold in the Soviet League.

3. Viacheslav Fetisov

Viacheslav Fetisov was often referred to as the Russian Bobby Orr. Unfortunately, by the time he was playing in the NHL (first for the Devils and later with the Red Wings), his scoring abilities were no longer part of his arsenal. Instead, Fetisov was an intelligent, rock-solid defender who rarely made mistakes and who came with a mean streak.

Earlier in his career, however, Fetisov was an offensive juggernaut. In the Soviet League where only one assist is awarded on goals, Fetisov regularly averaged a point per game during his 10 years with CSKA Moscow. With seven World Championships, two Olympic gold medals, and two Stanley Cups on his resumé, Fetisov accomplished just about everything a hockey player can.

But part of Fetisov's greatness is the man himself. Just as Bobby Orr changed the NHL by attacking from his defensive position and Patrick Roy changed goaltending by inventing the butterfly, Fetisov revolutionized Russian hockey by attacking when the opportunity was there and by jumping into the rush as the fourth attacker. Unlike Bobby Orr, Fetisov wasn't necessarily an end-to-end specialist. Despite his offensive instincts, he played a mean style of defense and was a tremendous passer who rarely coughed the puck up. In this sense, Fetisov played the game more like Denis Potvin or Nicklas Lidstrom than like Bobby Orr. Here is how Fetisov described his style:

> As a kid, nobody wants to play defense, everybody wants to score goals. But our system was pretty much strict with two defensemen and three forwards. But as a kid, I tried to find a way to score some goals, sneak through the back door or join the rush. I faced lots of criticism back then, but I stuck with my belief and kind of created a new system with offensive defensemen.

As this passage illustrates, Fetisov was always something of a non-conformer, which is a trait that didn't blend well with the Soviet hockey philosophy. In part, his individuality is what gave him the strength to play defense in new and different ways despite the criticism he received from coaches. This strength of character also served him well in the struggle Soviet players underwent in the mid to late '80s as they fought to gain the right to play NHL hockey.

While still in the Soviet Union, Fetisov publicly opposed totalitarian government and discussed some of the injustices he witnessed from coaches and administrators. He spoke about the general lack of freedom players had and the threats they faced. He was himself threatened with severe consequences for speaking out, such as banishment of his family to Siberia and false criminal charges.

Eventually, thanks to Gorbachev's perestroika movement in the late '80s, Fetisov won his battle for greater freedom. In 1989, he became one of the first Soviet citizens to receive a visa that allowed him to work in the West. That year, he played for the New Jersey Devils.

> *It was not easy. It sounds easy, but you always have to fight for everything and I fought for everything I have in hockey. I also won the biggest fight away from hockey. That was the fight against communism, the fight for freedom of choices.*

2. Vladislav Tretiak

Prior to the 1972 Summit Series, Canada sent a couple of scouts to Moscow to have a look at their competition. At the time, of course, neither team had much sense of how good their competition might be. Because of the lack of information entering the USSR, the Soviets likely knew next to nothing about the Canadian players. But this uncertainty was also one of the great intrigues leading up to the series.

In 1972, Tretiak was only 20 years old, and yet he was already recognized as the pre-eminent Soviet goaltender, having twice been named the Soviet League's best goalie. But Canada didn't know a thing about him; so when their scouts saw him let in eight goals during an inter-squad game, they wrongly assumed that he was weak, especially on the glove side. What the Canadian scouts didn't know was that Tretiak was getting married the next day and that he'd been out the night before ripping it up with some of the other guys on the team. As a result, Team Canada had no idea how good Tretiak was.

After letting in two early goals in the first game, the Big Red Machine came storming back and hammered the Canadians by the score of 7–3. From that point on, Tretiak had to earn his bacon, but by the time the Summit Series had concluded, no one doubted that Tretiak had put on one of the finest goaltending exhibitions of all-time. That same year, he led the Soviet Union to Olympic gold. In 1981, Tretiak was named the MVP of the Canada Cup.

1. Valery Kharlamov

Like Guy Lafleur in the 1970s, Wayne Gretzky in the '80s, Pavel Bure in the '90s and Ovechkin today, Valery Kharlamov had tremendous speed, soft hands, a cannon of a shot and the unpredictable ability to dipsy-doodle at full speed.

Of course, the first time Canadians saw Kharlamov play was during the Summit Series, when he was without question the Soviet Union's most lethal player. As the series wore on and tensions grew, Kharlamov continued to play phenomenal hockey, which is precisely why the Canadian brass sent Bobby Clarke on a mission to chop Kharlamov down. In game six, Clarke jumped over the boards and circled in behind Kharlamov. Clarke lifted his stick to the side and then chopped Kharlamov on the left ankle. Although Kharlamov finished the game, the slash had in fact fractured a bone in his ankle. He sat out game seven and was relatively ineffective in the decisive eighth game.

Unfortunately, Canada's victory and Paul Henderson's heroics should be measured against the fact that Canadian brutality prevented the most dangerous player in the series from playing the final two and a half games.

Aside from the Summit Series, Kharlamov has become, along with Tretiak, the biggest legend in

Soviet hockey. Much of the reason for this has to do with his personality and the way he played the game. Like many Soviet players who played under a military regime, Kharlamov's style is full of poetry and grace. "I love to play beautifully," Kharlamov once said in an interview.

According to Kharlamov's coach, the legendary Soviet strategist Anatoly Tarasov, there are three speeds to the game of hockey—the speed of moving, the speed of reflexes and the speed of thinking. Kharlamov mastered all three speeds.

Sadly, Kharlamov's life was as short as it was brilliant. In the spring of 1976, Kharlamov was seriously injured in a car accident, and although he returned to hockey and played four more seasons, the accident had taken the greatness from his game. Then, as if this first accident wasn't enough, another car accident in 1981 took his life. Valery Kharlamov was 33 years old.

Chapter Five

The Russian Generation

In the two decades since the initial infusion of Soviet-trained players, the NHL has become a truly global league. Over these 20 years, the impact of Russians has been tremendous, and their style of play has had a major role in transforming the North American game. The traditional smashmouth Canadian style that relies on will and physicality as much as skill has now merged with the Russian (not to mention other European nations) emphasis on skill and puck possession.

Although it remains true that Russian hockey players *tend* to have tremendous speed and skill whereas Canadians *tend* to be more robust, Alex Ovechkin is the most concrete example of a totally integrated hockey player. Although a few NHL stars possess a similar skill set, no hockey player in recent memory embodies both the Canadian and the Russian dimension as completely as

Ovechkin does. Like Eric Lindros, he is physically dominant, and like Pavel Bure, he has the speed and skill to score unbelievable goals while skating at top speed.

The following is a list of the Top 10 Russians of the post-Soviet era. Although Sergei Fedorov and Alexander Mogilny defected to North America just before the full collapse of the Soviet Union, we consider them part of the Russian hockey era, because they really were part of the second wave of Russian talent that followed players such as Larionov, Makarov and Fetisov.

Top 10 Russian Greats

10. Sergei Zubov

With a Stanley Cup ring to his credit, Sergei Zubov has a similar skill set to that of Sergei Gonchar. Both Zubov and Gonchar have perfected the art of quarterbacking a power-play unit. Although Zubov's career is now winding down, he has been one of the steadiest two-way defensemen over the past 15 years. A highly intelligent hockey player, Zubov rarely seems out of position, and he has always been one of the smoothest players in the game; he skates effortlessly, and his passes generally hit his target's stick on the tape in full stride. Although Zubov never really gained Norris Trophy consideration, his consistency and reliability speak volumes about the caliber of his game. In 1058 games with the Dallas Stars, Zubov recorded 767 points and an amazing overall plus-minus rating of +152.

9. Ilya Kovalchuk

When Ilya Kovalchuk came into the NHL in 2002, he was as flashy and reckless as Alex Ovechkin. Blessed with a diverse offensive arsenal, Kovalchuk took the NHL by storm, and he really hasn't let up. Unfortunately, Kovalchuk plays in the no-man's-land of Atlanta, where his accomplishments are easy to overlook. Despite scoring over 40 goals in five straight seasons, he has been overshadowed in the post-lockout era by Ovechkin, Sidney Crosby and Malkin, who play on better teams in more compelling hockey markets.

Nevertheless, Kovalchuk is an exhilarating player to watch—he has blazing speed, tremendous lateral mobility, a wicked wrist shot and a lethal one-timer. In this sense, his game is similar to Ovechkin's, though Kovalchuk isn't nearly as reckless in driving into traffic and towards the net as he was when he first broke into the league. But then again, when you're stuck in Atlanta playing for a perennial laughingstock, would you risk your body the way Ovechkin does?

8. Alexei Kovalev

Nicknamed *L'Artiste* by the French media in Montréal, Alexei Kovalev is a magician with the puck, and his ability to deke and fake is unparalleled. During his 16-year career, Kovalev has been a very productive player. Even though he has never topped 100 points or potted a 50-goal season, he is without a doubt one of the most talented players to ever play hockey. But because of his outrageous skills that regularly wow observers and embarrass opponents, Kovalev has often been portrayed as an underperformer. Although he won a Stanley Cup in 1994 with the New York Rangers, Kovalev has never moved into the upper echelon of NHL superstars, and many observers blame it on his personality and his on-ice work ethic.

But Kovalev is easy to misinterpret. Like Mario Lemieux, he often plays the game at a slower pace than he could, which is regularly misread as laziness. There is a subtlety to Kovalev's game that also accounts for the grace and beauty of the way he plays. By cruising through the neutral zone with the puck, he can often bring defenders out of position before dishing the puck to a teammate. His cruise-control speed is also capable of lulling defenders to sleep. He will then fake a pass or a shot, or pretend to accelerate wide before shifting inside on a dime. He is, in short, very tricky to read. On top of that, he's intelligent and independent, and he plays a Russian style of hockey that values puck possession and syncopated movement above all else.

In contrast to the Canadian brand of hockey, which emphasizes winning above style and individual hard work over collective chemistry, the Russian offensive style is like Brazilian soccer. Whereas Canadians and Americans tend to rely on desire and determination, Russian hockey has everything to do with collective unity. In international competition, Russian hockey is beautiful to watch for the simple reason that their puck possession develops a rhythm and a tempo that, once established, is easy for players to fit into and difficult for the opposition to disrupt. Furthermore, Russians rarely play dump-and-chase hockey because their philosophy encourages creative and instinctive behavior with the puck.

In the NHL context, though, North American fans often complain about Russians who look like they don't care. Kovalev and Alex Mogilny are two examples of stars who have had their character attacked for their apathy and laziness. In reality, the topsy-turvy careers of Mogilny and Kovalev serve to illustrate a tension in the hockey world that is very similar to multi-cultural tensions that surface every day in today's globalized world. In other words, Kovalev and Mogilny have been repeatedly misunderstood. Neither Mogilny nor Kovalev are lazy players. They simply struggle to adapt their talents to a style of play that is different from what they know. And for fans who desperately want their team to win, the knee-jerk reaction is to berate the players. But Kovalev has always been an accurate barometer for his team's chemistry, because when he's playing dominant hockey, it means his team is working like a well-oiled machine.

7. Pavel Datsyuk

Pavel Datsyuk is a classic Detroit Red Wing. Like Steve Yzerman and Sergei Fedorov before him, he is a dominant player at both ends of the rink, and yet his accomplishments and talents are often underrated or overlooked because of his unassuming personality. Just as Yzerman was often the second-best player in the league behind Wayne Gretzky and later Mario Lemieux, Datsyuk has an impact on the game all over the ice. In the past two years, Datsyuk has begun to earn greater accolades, and his two consecutive Selke trophies have solidified his reputation as the game's premier defensive forward. In the playoffs, Datsyuk also plays a crucial shutdown role as he always draws the assignment of going head-to-head against the opposition's most dangerous player.

Every year, Datsyuk also fills the stats sheet with consistent numbers. He scored 87 points in 2005–06 (75-28-59-87) and in 2006–07 (79-27-60-87), and then scored 97 points in 2007–08 (82-31-66-97) and in 2008–09 (81-32-65-97). As a result of his consistency, Datsyuk now seems to be garnering more attention for the brilliance of his all-around game—he was a finalist for the Hart Trophy as the NHL's MVP in 2008–09. Although the award rightfully went to Ovechkin for the second straight year, it isn't far-fetched to imagine that Datsyuk may soon win the award. After all, Nicklas Lidstrom didn't win his first Norris Trophy as the league's best defenseman until 2001—his 10th year in the league. Of course, it didn't help Lidstrom's case early in his career to play on a stacked lineup in Detroit, and Datsyuk is facing the same hurdle. Since winning his first award, though, Lidstrom has won the Norris six more times. Datsyuk, who is now 30 years old, also seems to be aging like fine wine, and when all is said and done, he could move into the upper echelon of Russian greats.

6. Sergei Gonchar

Sergei Gonchar has never been a dominant defensive defenseman, which is the only reason he's not any higher on this list. He has, however, gotten much steadier in his own zone as he has aged, and his offensive gifts are second to none. A superlative power-play quarterback who organizes the rush with patience and panache, Gonchar has one of the best one-timers in the game, and his passes rarely miss the mark. Now 35 years old, Gonchar still logs around 25 minutes per game, and by winning a Stanley Cup with Pittsburgh in 2009, he proved once again that he is an elite defenseman who plays just as well under pressure as he does during the regular season.

The 2009 playoffs also proved that Gonchar is a warrior who can battle through injury. In game four of Pittsburgh's series against Washington, Gonchar was deep in his own zone when he looked up and saw Ovechkin steaming towards him. At the last second, Gonchar stepped out of the way, but Ovechkin's knee collided with Gonchar's. The collision sent Gonchar spinning through the air before he landed awkwardly and writhed in pain. Ovechkin received a two-minute minor penalty on the play for kneeing, while Gonchar was helped off the ice with what was clearly a knee injury.

With such incidents, there is an inevitable conversation about a possible suspension in which the league commissioner (Colin Campbell) has to judge whether there was any intent to injure. Did Ovechkin stick out his knee or was the contact incidental? In this case, it is difficult to judge because it would have been a clean body check had Gonchar not stepped to the side. But because he did, the players' knees collided and Gonchar spun like a figure skater through the air, which made the hit look spectacular. Having said that, replays seem to confirm that Ovechkin continued on a straight path and never stuck his own knee out to purposely clip Gonchar. At any rate, this is how Colin Campbell saw the incident, and Ovechkin was not suspended.

Unfortunately, it turned out that Gonchar was injured on the play. He missed the next two games, but returned for the decisive game seven, which Pittsburgh won. After the game, Ovechkin, who is actually good friends with Gonchar off the ice, apologized for the hit: "I just tell him I didn't want to hit him. I just said 'sorry' and I explained what happened over there. Very good relation. I don't want to hit a guy to get him injured." However, once the playoffs were over and Gonchar had won his first Stanley Cup, it was revealed that he had played with a partially torn right medial collateral ligament.

5. Alexander Mogilny

Alex Mogilny was the first Russian hockey player to defect from the Soviet Union. In 1989, after the Soviet Union had won gold at the World Junior Championships in Anchorage, Alaska, Mogilny left his team and defected to North America with the help of representatives from the Buffalo Sabres, the NHL club that had drafted him.

In the Soviet Union, Mogilny had played for CSKA Moscow on a line that featured fellow prodigies Pavel Bure and Sergei Fedorov. The trio had also starred at the World Juniors in 1988 and 1989, and the Red Army had surely figured this line would replace the KLM line that had dominated the Soviet League throughout the 1980s. But that Red Army dream wasn't meant to be, and by defecting, Mogilny was taking a serious risk.

The Red Army, after all, groomed most of its players from a young age, which means that Mogilny had been a long-term investment, with CSKA having spent a great deal of time and money developing his skills. Also, unlike many of the other Soviet stars whose transfer had been negotiated with a significant portion of the players' salary going back to the Soviet club, CSKA didn't get anything for Mogilny.

In any case, after a tumultuous rookie season for the 20-year-old Mogilny, who struggled with the English language and a fear of flying, he started filling the net in the next few seasons. He scored 30 goals in 1990–91, 39 goals in 1991–92, and then in 1992–93, he busted out by scoring a mind-boggling 76 goals to tie Teemu Selanne for the league lead. In the 16 years since Mogilny and Selanne bulged the twine 76 times, no one has come close to duplicating the feat. Mogilny, though, remained a productive winger over the course of the next decade. After averaging over one point per game in his career (990-473-559-1032), Mogilny trails only Sergei Fedorov on the list of highest scoring Russians of all time.

Like Alexei Kovalev, though, Mogilny will be remembered as a talented player who could also be frustratingly enigmatic, if not downright lazy. In Vancouver, for example, Mogilny scored 55 goals in his first season, only to then fall off the charts over the next four seasons, scoring 31, 18, 14 and 21 goals, respectively. Mogilny, like many other Russian players, was a unique player who didn't necessarily need superstar linemates, but he certainly needed good chemistry with his linemates, as well as the team, in order to excel.

4. Evgeni Malkin

Who's better: Ovechkin or Malkin? Most fans and analysts seem to agree that, at this point in their careers, Ovechkin is a notch above Malkin, and Ovechkin's two consecutive MVP awards are the proof positive. But Malkin is not far off the pace. Although very different than Ovechkin in both style and personality, Geno (as he is commonly known in North America) is blossoming into perhaps the best all-around player in the world. Of course, he isn't the goal-scoring machine Ovechkin is, and, despite his imposing stature, Malkin doesn't play like a freight train.

Instead, Malkin is a playmaking centerman who has soft hands and the speed and power to drive to the net and finish in traffic. In the Penguins' championship season of 2008–09, Malkin not only led the NHL in scoring to win the Art Ross Trophy (82-35-78-113), but he also continued his stellar play right through the playoffs. After registering 36 points (24-14-22-36), Malkin became the first Russian player to win the Conn Smythe Trophy as the Playoff MVP. It also deserves to be mentioned that although Malkin often plays second fiddle to Sidney Crosby, he has proven over the last two years that he is, in fact, the better player. Of course, Crosby and Malkin help deflect a great deal of pressure from each other's shoulders, but in each of the past two seasons,

Malkin has been named Pittsburgh's regular-season MVP while leading his team in scoring both years.

Prior to joining the Penguins as a dominant 20-year-old rookie in 2006, Malkin had already played three years of world-class hockey for Metallurg Magnitogorsk in the Russian Super League. At that time, being a junior-age player, Malkin also showed the world how dominant he could be during the World Junior Championships. He played in three World Juniors and was often on a line with Alex Ovechkin. Together, the two Russian prodigies were virtually unstoppable. In 2005 and 2006, Malkin put up 10 points in six games, and both Malkin and Ovechkin looked like men among boys. After three seasons in Magnitogorsk, Malkin was ready to move on to the NHL, but the transfer from the Russian Super League to the NHL turned into a fiasco, and his career with the Penguins began after a dramatic (and highly publicized) escape from his Russian team.

The problem began just before the 2006–07 season when, after "immense psychological pressure," Malkin signed a one-year extension to remain in the Super League. The signing took place on August 7, 2006. Five days later, prior to the start of Metallurg's training camp in Helsinki,

Malkin left the team and was joined in Finland by his agent J.P. Barry.

At this point, it was revealed that the club had taken Malkin's passport to prevent him from leaving Finland and signing in Pittsburgh, where he clearly wanted to play. On August 15, a week after leaving his team, Malkin faxed a provision of a Russian labor law to authorities that enabled him to cancel his one-year contract by giving his employer two weeks' notice. Eventually, Malkin's passport was returned to him, and he was able to leave Finland.

The whole situation was a grim reminder of what it had been like 15 years earlier, when Soviet players such as Igor Larionov and Viacheslav Fetisov had spent years battling for their freedom from an oppressive Soviet military. Of course, Malkin's situation was dramatically different, and there was never really much of a threat to his personal freedom. But after listening to enough media speculation about what form this "psychological pressure" may have taken, it wasn't a stretch to wonder how involved the Russian mob was in the whole saga.

Aside from superficial parallels between the Soviet past and the Russian present, the greater issue that was brought to light during Malkin's dramatic escape was the growing tension between the RSL and the NHL. Since the turn of the millennium, the RSL (now the KHL) has become a significant force in the hockey market. As a result of the league's economic growth, Russian owners have started paying their players comparable salaries to what NHL teams pay. In other words, the NHL is no longer the only "money league," and in addition to the many Russians who have stayed at home instead of testing the NHL waters, more and more NHL players are looking at the KHL as another option—Jaromir Jagr, Ray Emery and Alexander Radulov being some of the more prominent examples.

Interestingly, the one-year contract Malkin signed with Magnitogorsk Metallurg was worth significantly more money than what he earned in his rookie season with the Pittsburgh Penguins. According to the new NHL Collective Bargaining Agreement (CBA) that was signed in 2005, entry-level players between the ages of 18 and 21 cannot earn a base salary of more than $925,000. Malkin's base salary in 2006–07 was $668,940, whereas Metallurg had signed him to a contract worth $3.45 million. In fact, in the fall of 2006, Malkin's former club filed an antitrust lawsuit against the Pittsburgh Penguins, the NHL and Malkin, stating that the Penguins' ownership group had signed Malkin while he was still under contract in Russia. The lawsuit also asserted that the NHL contract Malkin signed was "blatant and deliberate tampering and interference" with the contract he had signed in Russia. The claim was dismissed by the United States District Court.

In an ironic twist of fate, it was the NHL's turn to cry foul in 2008, after Alexander Radulov, a supremely talented young forward with the Nashville Predators, bailed on his NHL contract to sign a KHL contract. According to NHL Deputy Commissioner Bill Daly, "The bottom line from our perspective is that the player [Radulov] has a contract which our rules obligate him to respect. Our rules don't recognize a player [or his new team] being able to buy the way out of an existing contract. It's not a scenario that our existing rules contemplate or allow." The deal, however, was allowed to stand because it came a few days before a new transfer agreement was signed between the NHL and the KHL. The new transfer agreement provides each league with financial compensation based on the age of the player, how high he was drafted and a variety of other factors.

3. Pavel Bure

When Pavel Bure entered the NHL, he had the same basic effect on people as Ovechkin is now having. Quickly dubbed the Russian Rocket, Bure was far and away the most exciting thing to ever happen to the Vancouver Canucks franchise. Combining blazing speed with the ability to shift and deke at full speed, he had a personality and a skill set the NHL had never seen before.

As a junior player, Bure still holds the record for the most all-time goals at the World Junior Championships. Over the course of three World Juniors, Bure amassed 27 goals in only 21 games (21-27-12-39). In 1991, he made his debut with the Vancouver Canucks who, for the first time in their lowly history, were looking like a team on the rise. Arriving to much fanfare, Bure had little problem living up to the hype. Indeed, like Ovechkin, Bure had a flashy personality that was built for stardom. Despite missing the first month of the NHL season, Bure scored 34 goals, including a remarkable clip of 22 goals in the final 23 games of the season. He was awarded the Calder Trophy as the NHL's Rookie of the Year.

Over the course of his 13-year career, Pavel Bure was as pure a goal scorer as the NHL had ever seen. In an era that saw the invention of the "trap," a conservative defensive system that often made the game bland and boring, Bure put on a spectacle nearly every night. After his rookie season, Bure posted consecutive 60-goal campaigns prior to the 1995 lockout. In 1994, he also led Vancouver on a scintillating run to the Stanley Cup finals. Although the Canucks lost to the New York Rangers in a thrilling seven-game series, Bure had played brilliant hockey throughout the post-season, posting 31 points in 24 games (24-16-15-31).

Unfortunately, Bure's electrifying style took a toll on his body, and in particular his knees. When he rushed with the puck, Bure always seemed to be at full speed, and he had the rare ability to cut and shift, to move laterally to beat an opponent or to avoid a check. But when he was hit, he was often sent flying. At the beginning of the 1995–96 season, just after Vancouver had acquired Alexander Mogilny (which had Canuck fans imagining that they would be one of the most lethal duos in hockey history), Bure suffered a serious knee injury. A hit from Steve Smith tore Bure's anterior cruciate ligament, and he quickly went under the knife. This injury was the first of many, and although he managed three more 50-goal seasons, these were the only three years in which he played close to a full season.

In a way, it is sad to think that Bure's injuries were inevitable. He played the game with such boyish enthusiasm and reckless abandon that he was a joy to watch; and yet for opponents, the only way to stop him was to play him physically.

In a contact sport where players are often on the fence between playing clean or playing dirty, Bure's slight stature made him susceptible to taking head shots and knees from defensemen who occasionally chose the dirty route rather than get beat cleanly. Having said that, Pavel Bure was such a special player that in spite of his abbreviated career, he marked the NHL in a way that no one else had. But now we have Ovechkin, and the impact on the public imagination is remarkably similar.

2. Alexander Ovechkin

What separates Ovechkin from just about every other athlete is his infectious recklessness. Because of his youth—he is, after all, only 23 years old—Ovechkin seems to treat every opportunity to play as a gift that he wants to capitalize on every time he steps on the ice. In this regard, he is very much like Pavel Bure. The only real difference between the two is that Ovechkin is much bigger and more powerful, which allows him to dominate physically. But when the puck comes to Ovechkin or a turnover is created, he has the same explosive ability Bure had, and both players also loved scoring goals. But let's just keep our fingers crossed that Ovechkin's size allows him to get away with his frantic playing style.

After four years in the league, Ovechkin has missed a total of only three games. He has been a durable and physical point-producing stud who embraces and excels in every situation the game of hockey throws at him. With two straight Hart trophies on his mantle alongside four Kharlamov trophies as the best Russian player in the NHL, Ovechkin is the greatest thing to hit the NHL since Wayne Gretzky, which means that in four short years, his impact has been more significant than that of Mario Lemieux, Eric Lindros, Pavel Bure and even Sidney Crosby.

1. Sergei Fedorov

Although Alex Ovechkin, Evgeni Malkin and Pavel Datsyuk may surpass Fedorov by the time all is said and done, Sergei Fedorov had a legendary NHL career that finally came to an end after the 2008–09 season, his 18th in the league.

Although some may argue that Fedorov didn't have the same impact on the NHL as Pavel Bure or Alex Ovechkin, the fact that he played a central role during three Stanley Cup runs in Detroit puts him at the head of the class. At the end of the day, greatness must be measured by team success as well as individual accomplishments, and the reason team success plays such a vital role is that the pressure-packed situations that teams contend with in the playoffs help test a player's fortitude.

In Fedorov's case, he excelled in a wide variety of roles, and although Detroit clearly had great teams, Fedorov was the best all-around player in hockey for a couple of years. His big season was 1993–94, when his 120 points (82-56-64-120) earned him the Hart Trophy as the NHL MVP. After the lockout-shortened 1994–95 season, Fedorov had another outstanding offensive season by posting 107 points (78-39-68-107). Despite long playoff runs in 1995 and 1996 when Fedorov was at his offensive peak, it wasn't until 1997 that Detroit won the Stanley Cup. In 1998, they won it again, and then again in 2002. During each of these runs, Fedorov averaged roughly a point per game, registering 20 points in 1997 (20-8-12-20), 20 points in 1998 (22-10-10-20) and 19 points in 2002 (23-5-14-19).

Over the past few years, fans will remember Fedorov as more of a defensive specialist than an offensive dynamo. But even this is a testament to Fedorov's overall game and his willingness to serve the team. Throughout the 1990s, Fedorov was more or less like Pavel Datsyuk is today. A highly skilled centerman who twice won the Selke Trophy as the NHL's best defensive forward, Fedorov was a great faceoff man, killed penalties, played on the first-unit power play, averaged over 20 minutes a game and was usually on the ice in the final minute. But as his career wore on, Fedorov shifted seamlessly into a more defensive role.

In his final year in the NHL, it was indeed fitting that Fedorov played in Washington as something of a mentor figure for Alex Ovechkin. Although Fedorov wasn't quite the media sensation Ovechkin is turning out to be, his experience and professionalism have no doubt rubbed off on Ovechkin. Now 39 years old, Fedorov signed a two-year contract with Metallurg Magnitogorsk of the KHL, where he will play with his brother Fedor. He is leaving the NHL as the highest scoring Russian in NHL history. In 1248 games, Fedorov piled up 483 goals, 696 assists and 1179 points.

Chapter Six

The Highlight Reel

The term "human highlight reel" is often bandied about willy-nilly in the sports world to describe superlative athletes who produce highlight-worthy material on a regular basis. Alex Ovechkin is one of those athletes. He is a pure goal scorer with a lightning-quick release, but he is unique because he steamrolls defenders and finishes in traffic. He has breakaway speed, but he is spectacular because of his creativity while flying at full speed. Ovechkin also never gives up on a play. He might lose the puck in his skates or get knocked to the ice by a defender, but some of Ovechkin's most celebrated goals have been scored from the seat of his pants or while falling to the ice. Here is a countdown of his five most remarkable efforts, all of which have been played millions of times on TV highlight reels and on YouTube.

Top Five Goals

5. The Anaheim Goal

Washington Capitals vs. Anaheim Ducks
January 13, 2006
Washington won 3–2 in overtime

Although Ovechkin has one of the hardest and most accurate shots in the game today, the reason he makes highlight reels on a weekly basis is that he has an incredible repertoire of moves that he performs at full speed. In addition to his tremendous skill set, Ovechkin also plays with a dogged determination to fight for the puck in traffic and to regularly make plays while falling down or spinning seemingly out of control.

This latter trait was certainly put on display during a 2006 contest in Anaheim. After a Caps' winger had created a turnover along the boards in the Ducks' zone, Ovechkin swooped in to pick up the garbage. As he darted into the slot, Ruslan Salei came towards him, only to start back-pedaling when Ovechkin went wide. Ovechkin tried to play the puck through Salei's skates, but hit one of the defenseman's skates. While still moving around Salei, Ovechkin fished the puck free, but by the time he had regained control, he was nearly at the icing line and had no angle for a shot. Ever the magician, Ovechkin spun around and, after a full 360, he blindly fired the puck at the

Anaheim goal. As luck would have it, the puck found the far corner.

4. The Rangers Goal

New York Rangers vs. Washington Capitals
April 24, 2009
Washington won 4–0

In the opening round of the 2009 Stanley Cup playoffs, the Washington Capitals were facing the New York Rangers. Going into game five, the Caps were trailing three games to one. But game five proved to be the turning point in the series. With the crowd in Washington already going ballistic with their beloved Caps up 3–0, Ovechkin pounced on a loose puck inside his own blue line and was off to the races.

As he powered through the neutral zone, Ovechkin was facing two Blueshirts. He carried the puck wide to one side, and then cut towards the center of the ice. Chris Drury, who was back-checking on the play, cut towards Ovechkin and tried to knock his head off, but Ovechkin, with his head up, side-stepped the check. Then, with Derek Morris stepping up and fishing for the puck, Ovechkin dragged the puck through Morris' legs and cut around him, now with a clear path to the net. For a moment, he lost the puck in his skates, but at the last second, Ovechkin kicked it up to his stick and, while falling to the ground, slapped a backhand through Henrik Lundqvist's five-hole. The goal not only finished the Rangers that night, but Washington also went on to win the series in seven electrifying games.

3. The Buffalo Goal
Buffalo Sabres vs. Washington Capitals
December 26, 2008
Washington won 3–2

Like a few of his more incredible and memorable goals, Ovechkin's beauty against Buffalo was scored after he was knocked to the ice. On this play, Buffalo had control of the puck deep in Washington's zone. The Sabres were trailing 2–1 midway through the third period; the play started when a Sabres' player shot the puck towards the net. The puck was then knocked down and thrown towards the blue line, where Ovechkin picked it up.

One of Ovechkin's great assets is the tremendous leg drive he has, which allows him to accelerate at an incredible rate. He also has a Gretzky-like sense for where the puck will be, which helps him find open ice despite the attention he inevitably receives from the opposition. In this case, as soon as the puck was knocked down in front of the net, Ovechkin bolted from his defensive responsibility along the boards. As he sliced towards the center of the ice, the puck found him, and off he went.

As a defender, it must be frightening to find yourself in a one-on-one situation against Ovechkin, especially when he has two-thirds of the rink to work with. This was the situation Henrik Tallinder was facing. A steady if unspectacular defenseman, Tallinder was in a bad position to deal with Ovechkin. Instead of being directly in front of him, Tallinder, who'd been patrolling the left point, immediately turned and tried to cut Ovechkin off. Ovechkin, meanwhile, was pounding down the ice like bull in a china shop. At the Sabres' blue line, Tallinder, who'd taken a good angle, skated in front of Ovechkin and tried to knock the puck off his stick. But Ovechkin saw Tallinder's angle, and despite his own speed, Ovechkin managed to play the puck through Tallinder's skates. Now alone in the slot and facing Buffalo goalie Patrick Lalime, Ovechkin began to fall as he battled to stay ahead of Tallinder who was in hot pursuit. As Ovechkin dove forward, he snapped the puck through Lalime's five-hole and went crashing into the goalie's pads. The goal worked as an insurance marker, putting the Caps ahead 3–1.

2. The Montréal Goal

Montréal Canadiens vs. Washington Capitals
February 18, 2009
Washington won 4–3 in a shoot-out

Ovechkin has talked on a number of occasions about his love for the hockey hotbeds across Canada. As a kid who welcomes the spotlight and often plays his best hockey when it is shining brightly on him, Ovechkin has had a few scintillating performances in both Montréal and Toronto. In 2009, he tore Montréal to shreds.

On January 31, Ovechkin scored four goals against the Habs in a game that went into overtime. The game had been a physical run-and-gun affair, a style that Ovechkin relishes. With the game tied at three in the third period, Ovechkin scored the go-ahead goal, and it appeared the Caps would hang on; but with just over 30 seconds to play, Montréal tied the score and sent the game into overtime. In the extra frame, Ovechkin quite naturally supplied the heroics by scoring the game winner.

After that game in Washington, the two teams met less than a month later for a highly anticipated rematch. With Montréal leading the game 1–0 midway through the first, Ovechkin came onto the ice as the Canadiens were moving out of their own zone. After an errant pass between defensemen bounced off the boards at center ice, Ovechkin beat Roman Hamrlik to the loose puck and chipped it past the Habs' veteran defense-man. Hamrlik, realizing he'd lost the race, tried to throw a hip check to slow Ovechkin down. But after chipping the puck off the boards, Ovechkin spun 360° around Hamrlik, picked the puck up at the Montréal blue line and raced towards the net. Kyle Chipchura, who was chasing from behind, met Ovechkin at the faceoff dot and tried to knock the puck off Ovechkin's stick. But Ovechkin absorbed the contact, using his body to shield the puck. As he slid past Chipchura, Ovechkin fell to the ice and slid on the seat of his pants towards Carey Price and across the goalmouth. While sliding on his backside and before crashing heavily into Price, Ovechkin had the presence of mind and the strength to lift the puck over Price's right pad and into the back of the net.

1. The Phoenix Goal

Washington Capitals vs. Phoenix Coyotes
January 16, 2006
Washington won 6–1

Among hockey fanatics, there is some debate about which goal was more miraculous: the Phoenix Goal or the Montréal Goal. But as stunning a display of skill and power as the

Montréal Goal was, the goal Ovechkin scored in his rookie season in Phoenix was flat-out miraculous. It also proved the old hockey adage that you have to be good to be lucky.

On January 16, 2006, as a 20-year-old rookie en route to winning the Calder Trophy as the NHL's Rookie of the Year, Ovechkin scored a goal for the ages. The game was in Phoenix, and with the Great One, Wayne Gretzky, coaching his Coyotes through another dismal performance, Ovechkin took center stage.

Picking the puck up at center ice, Ovechkin came into the attacking zone one-on-one against the Coyotes' Paul Mara. Skating diagonally from left to right, Ovechkin went directly into Mara's body, with his eyes still on the puck. Mara got his gloves into Ovechkin's face, and as Ovechkin reached the slot, Mara knocked Ovechkin to the ground. But as he fell away from the defender, Ovechkin twisted through the air and landed on his back. Amazingly, as he slid farther away from the goal, he managed to cradle the puck with the toe of his stick and fling the puck towards the net. The Phoenix goalie, meanwhile, had wandered way out of his crease, leaving him in no-man's-land between the play and his net. Despite the poor positioning, Ovechkin was about 10 feet from the net and lying directly on his back when he released the puck with one hand on his stick. Unbelievably, it found the corner of the net.

And how did Ovechkin celebrate one of the greatest goals in hockey history? In typical Ovi fashion, the second he saw the goal was in, he jumped to his feet, skated along the boards, dropped to one knee and gave the crowd a wheeling, left-handed fist pump. Then he kissed his glove and raised it towards the Phoenix bench. The whole show was beautiful and jaw-dropping.

After the game, when asked if it was the best goal he'd ever scored, Ovechkin had this to say,

> *That was lucky. Best score? Oh yeah. I just went down and try shoot and score goal. [Chris] Clark came to me and said, "You scored!" and I said, "Wow!" I saw replay: it was beautiful.*

Shortly thereafter, when Coyotes coach Wayne Gretzky was asked about Ovechkin and his game, he said,

> *I've got to tell you, I love the kid. He's the only guy I've ever coached against who scored a goal and blew me a kiss. Pretty good goal, too. You can see he loves to play.*

Chapter Seven

Broadcasting Alexander the GR8

The Russian Machine

No one has ever played hockey quite like Alex Ovechkin. There have been power forwards who played smashmouth hockey and scored like Wilt "the Stilt" Chamberlain—Gordie Howe, Cam Neely and Jarome Iginla come to mind; there have been bullies like Bobby Clarke, Mark Messier and Eric Lindros, whose attitude and raw physicality instilled fear in opponents; and there have been speed demons like Bobby Hull, Guy Lafleur and Pavel Bure, who thrilled fans with electrifying end-to-end rushes. But can you think of anyone else who would charge down the wing like a wild stallion and throw offensive body checks when a defenseman cuts across to lower the boom?

For the sake of comparison, Eric Lindros is the only other player who attacked like a freight train when carrying the puck. Like Ovechkin, he was just as likely to plow *through* the defenseman as he was to take it wide with speed or to deke you out of your jockstrap. But Ovechkin is already a more dynamic player than Lindros ever was. Lindros was a fairly straightforward player. Even in the prime of his early 20s when Lindros centered the so-called Legion of Doom line with John Leclair and Mikael Renberg, Lindros' game was all about physical superiority.

For a while, he was dominant; in the lockout-shortened season of 1995, at the age of 22, he won the Hart Trophy as the NHL's MVP. But after an open-ice collision with Darius Kasparaitis on March 7, 1998, Lindros suffered a few concussions, and he struggled to adapt—in part because his game was fairly one-dimensional.

Then, in a pivotal playoff game the following year, in his second game back after being side-lined with post-concussion syndrome, Lindros met the Scott Stevens Express. It was game seven of the Eastern Conference Finals, and Lindros had just picked up a loose puck at center ice. As he came over the Devils' blue line and cut inside, Stevens, who specialized in throwing clean shoulder checks on players who had their heads down, caught Lindros fishing for the puck. The hit dropped Lindros immediately, and the Devils went on to win the game and eventually the Stanley Cup.

After the notorious Stevens hit, Lindros played a few more seasons, but he was a shadow of his former self. In his prime, he had been a thoroughbred who was built on power; even though he still had the power after his first concussion, the sad truth is that he needed to change his style in order to avoid the downward spiral that often comes with repeated head injuries.

It is one of the tragic aspects of the modern game that the NHL has failed to address the ongoing concussion issue in a serious way. For years, the euphemism "concussion-like symptoms" has been used for what could also be called "mild brain damage" to describe the lingering effects that are often part and parcel of suffering a concussion.

So far, the answer from NHL Commissioner Gary Bettman and his minions has been to "crack down on head shots." What this means in the hockey realm is both unclear and very slippery. As players continue to grow in size and speed, hitting in general has become more spectacular—which, of course, the fans love—and much more dangerous. Finishing checks in the NHL is rarely a matter of just riding a player into the boards; in today's game, it is the duty of third- and fourth-line grinders to change a game's momentum by throwing spectacular hits. The hits may be borderline dirty, but anything that gets the crowd involved is generally considered worth the risk of the occasional penalty.

But it is becoming increasingly obvious that the human brain can't stand the impact of a crushing shoulder check to the head. Open-ice collisions are like head-on car accidents—they are explosive and dangerous.

Hits from behind can be just as bad, since the victim often gets his head or face driven into the unforgiving Plexiglas.

Finally, there is the bone-crushing variety of body check in which a forechecking player comes flying at the puck carrier and "finishes his check" by driving the player who has just released the puck into the boards as hard as he can. Although these hits are much more frequent than open-ice collisions, the impact on shoulders can be damaging, and if you try to sidestep the hit, the leg is often the last part of the body to step aside, which leaves the knee exposed and very vulnerable.

A good example is the knee-on-knee hit that occurred in the 2009 second-round playoff series between Washington and Pittsburgh when Ovechkin came in to hit his good buddy Sergei Gonchar.

As Don Cherry (bless his old and judgmental heart) has pointed out on a number of occasions, part of the problem lies in the hard plastic used in today's shoulder and elbow pads. Pads are, of course, designed to protect the player, but it would be naïve to ignore the fact that they double as weapons. At the risk of sounding like a homer, in the good ol' days, or let's say in Gretzky's era, players wore very light padding made from various fibers, but only helmets, jocks and shin pads used hard industrial plastics.

So even when you were battling in the corner against Messier and he caught you on the chin with a quick jab of the elbow, the worst-case scenario was that you might lose a couple of chicklets and need a few snorts of smelling salts. The same goes for an open-ice hit. In the early '80s, when Rod Langway caught you with your head down, he'd usually flatten you like a pancake, but you weren't really in danger of having cobwebs and behaving like a zombie for the next few months.

Today, padding is more like a knight's armor, and the elbow and shoulder pads are particularly problematic because hitting brings them into play. If a player has his head down and he's fishing for the puck, a clean shoulder check might not only knock a few teeth out, it might also rearrange a few brain cells.

The speed and size of players is also a contributing factor, and so is the player's intention when delivering a hit. It is rare to see players let up when another player is in a vulnerable position, and more and more seemingly clean hits are resulting in concussions, separated shoulders and knee injuries.

Scott Stevens provides the best illustration of the problem. When he retired in 2004, Stevens had knocked many players into oblivion, and yet he had only received four elbowing penalties during his brilliant 22-year NHL career. It is remarkable to think that one of the game's most dangerous open-ice hitters always threw clean body checks. He never left his feet, and he rarely brought his elbow up. And yet players occasionally left the ice with concussions.

Nowadays, little guys like Colby Armstrong are legally hitting other players, leading with their shoulder and not leaving their feet, yet bodies are still dropping like flies. In 2007–08, there were 760 man-games lost because of concussions and concussion-related symptoms, which include such lingering effects as migraine headaches, memory loss, dizzy spells, fatigue and depression. According to an *Orange*

County Register study of NHL injuries over the past 10 years, the 760 man-games lost represented a whopping 41 percent increase over the previous year.

Prior to the 2008–09 season, Dr. Charles Tator, a professor of neurosurgery at the University of Toronto, had this to say when asked about the growing epidemic of head injuries in the NHL:

> *Is it going to take a death to make the NHL see the problem? The owners and the NHL have absolutely turned a blind eye to head injuries.*

The reason for raising the issue of hits leading to concussions is that Alex Ovechkin is a high-risk player. He plays hockey with reckless abandon, which is both his beauty and his potential Achilles' heel. Injuries are a part of the game, and anyone can suffer them. But over the past couple of decades, many of the NHL's budding stars have fallen from greatness and glory.

In today's game, it seems only natural for young players who have the skill set to do amazing things at full speed to run into headhunters. Just think of Pavel Bure's knee injuries and the concussions of Eric Lindros and Pat Lafontaine. These are three of the more memorable cases of dominant NHL players whose bodies couldn't take the punishment. At the time of their respective injuries, all three were elite players, but injury brought them down to earth.

With Ovechkin, everyone fears for his health. As Don Cherry once predicted on "Coach's Corner," the time may come for some hulking defenseman to crush the greatness out of Ovechkin. Then again, maybe Ovechkin is strong enough to withstand all comers. If you ask him about the potential for injury, his opinion is that "Russian machine never breaks."

Despite Ovechkin's faith in his own genetic strength, the question of his durability is one that fans fear to some extent, and that the Washington Capitals and the NHL fear much more.

As we will see in a variety of ways throughout this chapter, Ovechkin is a marketing dream come true. From a branding perspective, Ovechkin is the engine that drives the Capitals franchise. Prior to his arrival, the Capitals were knocking on death's door. Like the bland kid in school that no one ever noticed, Washington had been an irrelevant team throughout much of its 30-year history before Ovechkin came on board. But when he entered the fray, the Washington Capitals morphed into a credible brand. Ovechkin T-shirts and jerseys sell like hotcakes, and, more significantly, the Capitals logo has slowly shifted its meaning in the public imagination. Today, instead of negatively affiliating the Caps icon with futility, the average hockey fan positively associates Washington with Ovechkin, which in turn means spectacular, exciting and cool.

The Rock-Star Complex

Anyone can have a rock-star complex. It is as simple as believing in your own greatness and relishing public attention. Most of the time, people with rock-star complexes believe their own status or fame puts them in a privileged social position. Since money and fame are the two keys to social power in contemporary Western culture, many people have great difficulty handling their new-found power.

As is so often the case with genuine rock stars, the ego trip of buying into the idea of your own greatness often leads to extreme and self-destructive behavior. For young men like Alexander Ovechkin, it takes great strength to remain on an even keel when everyone wants a piece of your time or your money.

Alexander Ovechkin may have a rock-star complex, but it remains to be seen how destructive it becomes. As he likes to say, "It's good to be Ovi," and how can you argue with that? After all, he is a Russian kid who's living the American

Dream at full throttle. Within four years, he has proven himself to be the best player in today's game. He drives fancy sports cars, has the largest contract in NHL history, dates gorgeous women and wears designer clothes. In other words, he's living the life most people can only fantasize about. The trouble is that such a lifestyle is unsustainable, and it will be interesting to see how Ovechkin deals with adversity when it comes.

In the past, we have seen many superstars rise to the occasion and handle the media scrutiny and public expectation seamlessly. Wayne Gretzky and Michael Jordan are perhaps the two examples par excellence. By no stretch of the imagination were either of them perfect, but they remained athletic icons well into their retirement in large part because their professional success didn't cause their personal downfall. In other words, neither Jordan nor Gretzky turned into self-destructive rock stars.

Diego Maradona, on the other hand, is a classic example of the pitfalls of buying into the rock-star complex. Revered by an adoring public in the Catholic lands of Argentina and Italy, Maradona fuelled myths in the zealous minds of his followers and the collective psyche of his country. But he was too good for his own good.

A soccer genius, Maradona rose from the slums of Buenos Aires to become an icon and an idol in Argentina and Italy. Author of the infamous Hand of God goal that he punched in against England during the 1986 World Cup, many of Maradona's goals were the result of his trademark end-to-end rushes. He was like watching Ovechkin in a short-shorts and a pair of Adidas. But Maradona was given to excess. Derailed multiple times for cocaine violations and banned from the 1994 World Cup because of an ephedrine-tainted urine sample, Maradona fell off the world stage in tragic fashion. Despite his collapse, he has remained in the Latin American spotlight well into his retirement—whether as a clown, a talking head or a tribal god is unclear.

Unlike Diego Maradona, Alexander Ovechkin grew up in a relatively stable situation in Moscow. His parents both worked, and he has inherited his mother's bull-headed determination. But fame has a way of changing people, so let's all have faith in Ovechkin's strength of character. Let's believe that Ovechkin will not be distracted by the seductive power of fame and celebrity. After all, as his mother once flatly pointed out, "He doesn't have the stardom disease. People who say these things are jealous."

The Golf Cart Incident and Ovechkin's Need for Speed

On the ice, Alexander Ovechkin is more reckless than a Judas Priest guitar solo. Off the ice, he's pretty much the same. In June 2008, the day after being the first Washington Capital to ever win the Hart Trophy as the NHL's MVP, Ovechkin was awarded a symbolic key to the city of Washington by Mayor Adrian M. Fenty.

"It's a big honor to stand here today," Ovechkin said with a massive gap-toothed grin on his face. "Thank you for your support. You are unbelievable, guys. I love you."

But as polite and sincere as Ovechkin can be, he is also a kid who loves to have fun. Despite his limited English, he always manages to convey his sense of humor. So with 500 or so fans chanting "M-V-P, M-V-P," Ovechkin, who is known for his love of speeding around town in exotic sports cars, got a little cocky:

> *Today is a big day; I have key for the city.*
> *I am president this day in the city. For one*
> *day. So everybody have fun and no speed*
> *limit tickets!*

In real life, Ovechkin is a rich young man who lives (and apparently drives) with reckless abandon. As an example of his recklessness, there is a behind-the-scenes video that made its way online (and then went viral) in which Ovechkin and Mike Green are horsing around on an equipment cart in the halls of the Verizon Center where Washington plays their home games. In the video, Ovechkin is driving, Green is sitting beside him, and they've decided to race towards a large floor-to-ceiling door that closes by dropping from the ceiling to the floor.

So with Ovechkin and Green sitting in their equipment cart about 50 feet away from the door when it starts to close, Ovechkin floors it, and the cart speeds towards the closing door. As they get closer to the door, things start to look dicey; the cart will probably clear, but what about Ovechkin and Green? It looks like they might get their heads lopped off! In the end, Green drops his head to escape the quickly dropping door, while Ovechkin drives straight through and has to lean back, his head just barely scraping by.

On the road, Ovechkin has a few sports cars, and the most recent addition to his collection is a Mercedes SL AMG Black Series, an uber-rare model that only 350 people in the world own. How was he able to get his hands on such a rare vehicle, you ask? "Because I'm Ovi," Ovechkin answers with a grin. But despite his power, money and fame, Ovi is a kid, and he behaves that way, which is why he is so universally admired.

Unlike the even-keeled Sidney Crosby, who acts like a weathered veteran who went to the Gretzky school of diplomacy, Ovechkin plays hockey and lives his life like a kid. His energy and enthusiasm are infectious.

When asked about his driving habits, Ovechkin says rather casually, "Here I drive 160 miles. In Russia, I put max, like 220, 240, probably." Then, when asked whether he thinks he needs to stop, Ovechkin gets downright philosophical:

> *My dad say, "Don't think about tomorrow, think about right now: if you want to do something, do it."*

The Capitals' brass, on the other hand, has expressed their concern regarding Ovechkin's reckless habits on the road. And there's no question that Ovechkin must be intoxicated with the belief that he is superhuman. After all, the media and fans shower him with so many accolades that it must be virtually impossible to feel limited in any meaningful way by something so seemingly obscure as his mortality.

Besides these concerns, Ovechkin also has a personal reason to slow down. There is a remarkable history of car accidents in the Ovechkin family, to the extent that one is compelled to see a degree of tragic irony in the fact that he is hooked on speed. At the age of seven, Ovechkin's mother, Tatiana, was hit by a passing car, and Alex's older brother Sergei died from complications stemming from a car accident.

With such a tragic history, Ovechkin's love of cars is truly astounding, and it provides even more proof that Ovechkin just attacks life without worrying about the consequences.

Branding Ovechkin

Every year, *Forbes* magazine publishes a review of all types of businesses, including NHL franchises. Although they have yet to release their 2009 report, the 2008 report shows the impact Ovechkin has had on Washington's bottom line.

In 1999, current owner Ted Leonsis bought the Capitals franchise for $85 million. After the 2008 season in which Ovechkin carried the Caps back to the playoffs and won the NHL's MVP title (becoming the first Washington sports player to win an MVP award since Redskins' quarterback Joe Theismann was the NFL MVP way back in 1983), the Capitals franchise was valued at $160 million, its highest mark since *Forbes* began tracking NHL teams 10 years ago. By comparison, in 2007, the Capitals were valued at only $127 million, the lowest value of any NHL franchise, including such sad-sack organizations as the New York Islanders and the Phoenix Coyotes, who now represent the lowest ranking teams.

During the 2007–08 season, driven by the allure of Ovechkin, attendance at Verizon Center rose by 12 percent, and TV ratings more than doubled. In a lukewarm hockey market like Washington, this is truly something to cheer about.

As a general standard, a team's value can be roughly measured by doubling the current year's revenue. In Washington's case, their revenue increased from $66 million in 2006–07 to $73 million in 2007–08. Of course, the $73 million revenue still represents one of the lowest in the league, and despite the $33 million jump in the team's valuation from 2007 to 2008, the Capitals remain near the bottom of the league, ranked 26th out of 30 teams.

From the NHL's standpoint, the budding rivalry between Sidney Crosby and Alex Ovechkin is like money in their pocket. Although no landmark TV deals have been signed with big-league American broadcasters, NHL bigwigs are banking on the Ovechkin-Crosby rivalry to fuel further American interest in the game.

During the 2009 second-round playoff series between the Penguins and the Capitals, TV ratings in the U.S. skyrocketed. In particular, the legendary game-two showdown in which Crosby and Ovechkin each recorded a hat trick drew 1.2 million viewers, the highest total for a second-round game in seven years. On the whole, the TV ratings for the series were 18 percent higher than the previous year.

Still, the fact that Ovechkin plays in a relatively minor hockey market limits his marketability. Although his play is contributing to the NHL's pursuit of a bigger American TV deal, some marketing gurus see some problems with Ovechkin's commodification. The following quotation is from Bob Stellick, president of Stellick Marketing Communications Inc., a firm that specializes in hockey and other sports:

> *Ovechkin certainly has enthusiasm and personality as his greatest assets. With the Capitals having some success this year, it has certainly helped his profile. However, his English skills and the fact that Washington is not a major U.S. market team—like New York, Chicago, L.A., or Boston—doesn't help. Gretzky's main success as a sponsorable property was in Canada. He certainly received some awareness in the*

U.S. because hockey was on the rise and he was playing in L.A., but it was still difficult for him to crack into the major leagues of U.S. sponsorships. There are just too many NFL, MLB, NBA, and Nascar types who play in sports with significantly higher profiles than hockey.

The way Bob Stellick qualifies Ovechkin's potential as a "sponsorable property" is a sad reflection of the advertising madness that is inevitably imposed upon the rich and the famous.

Ovechkin has appeared in a few TV ads, and his largest deals are with Verizon Wireless and with CCM, who have created a new brand of apparel called the Ovechkin Designer Street Wear Collection.

But Ovechkin's unique personality makes him a little tricky to turn into a long-term product spokesman the way Wayne Gretzky has been for Ford or Michael Jordan has been for Nike. But perhaps this is more of a blessing than a curse.

The Motherlode

When Ovechkin signed a contract extension with the Washington Capitals in 2008, it was the richest contract in NHL history. Two years earlier, Ovechkin had fired his long-time agent Don Meehan and replaced him with his mother,

Tatiana. Long before he was an NHL player, Meehan had represented Ovechkin's interests. But after five years together, Ovechkin cut his ties with Meehan. At the time, Ovechkin was 21 years old, and it seemed like an odd decision given Meehan's respectability and his wealth of NHL experience.

From the Ovechkin perspective, though, Tatiana Ovechkina is the president of the Moscow Dynamo women's basketball team, which means she is used to haggling over numbers, even if she usually sits on the other side of the table. In representing her son, she was a tough negotiator.

"I wouldn't call her uncompromising because she did, in fact, compromise," Capitals' general manager George McPhee said about the contract negotiation. "But Alex's mother is very strong, very protective. And she knows what she wants." In the end, Ovechkin signed a 13-year deal worth $124 million. The deal pays Ovechkin $9 million in each of the first six years, and $10 million per season over the remaining seven.

In a *Sports Illustrated* article by Michael Farber that details how the deal went down, he had this to say about the partnership between mother and son:

If Alexander technically represented himself in arranging the NHL's first nine-figure deal, he made no move without Tatiana's approval. She is not nominally her son's agent. She is so much more. She is the matriarch, the progenitor of her son's extraordinary athletic genes, his intractable resolve and his jersey number—Alexander wears number 8, the same as she did. Tatiana gives her son love, counsel, toughness and dinner.

Facebook Junkies

You know you're in the 21st century when a 23-year-old kid from Moscow can come to America, show his face on a website and garner more than 59,000 "fans." Of course, the hockey gods blessed him with an insatiable appetite for scoring goals, and the way Alex Ovechkin carries and expresses himself makes it difficult not to call yourself a fan.

But just like Facebook "friends," there's nothing legitimate about being a Facebook "fan" of Ovechkin. First of all, Ovechkin himself has nothing to do with his own profile. He doesn't chat with his fans, he doesn't write on his own wall, and he doesn't even add his own status updates. And why would he? Can you imagine any multimillion-dollar hockey stud taking the time to chat with his 59,696 (and counting) fans?

In fact, if you were ever to meet the man, you'd likely grovel like a schoolboy, mumbling inaudibly as you ransack your backpack in desperate search of a writing instrument and a wrinkled scrap of paper.

Being an Ovechkin "fan" on Facebook really means that you want to belong, and so, in an effort to feel socially in tune, you follow Ovechkin's profile so that you can discuss with other Ovechkin "fans" how great he is. And there's nothing wrong with wanting to belong. After all, most of our parents, or more likely our grandparents, used church as the social vehicle to derive a sense of belonging. Today, the main medium for young men is sports.

Like most "fans," you idly register yourself as a "fan" as an addendum to your own Facebook profile, thereby earning you a penny of social capital among your own cybernetic "friends." Or, if you happen to be as eager in the digital world as Ovechkin is in real life, perhaps you even resort to socializing with other Ovechkin "fans" on his "wall," where you can post comments that might begin a dialogue among other Ovechkin freaks.

Katja: The Internet Girlfriend

In February 2008, Sasha met Katja. They met through the online site Odnoklassniki.ru, which is basically the Russian version of Facebook. The word "odnoklassniki" means "classmates," and it is a social networking site that brings old and new friends together. Amazingly, an online relationship developed that turned into a real-life romance.

The following excerpt is from a transcript of an interview Katja gave the Russian newspaper *Soviet Sport*; it was translated and appeared in its current form on the weblog AlexOvetjkin.blogspot.com:

> *One day* [Sasha] *said, "We are leaving for a road trip. I am asking you a favor to give me your phone number." I gave him the phone and the next morning a text from him "Hi! This is my American phone number." And our infinite text correspondence has started from there, you can write down another novel about it. You won't believe it, we text to each other every half hour! He'd send me text 10 minutes before the start of the game, and even in between during the breaks. "Thinking of you" or "Honey, I scored this goal in your honor."*
>
> *And he called me... We talked for 2 hours every day.*

Like most romances between young people in their early 20s, the romance between Katja and Sasha was short-lived. But it does show that Ovechkin is a regular dude who is looking for love just like the rest of us.

Inside Hockey

During the 2009 NHL playoffs, *Hockey Night in Canada*'s pre-game feature "Inside Hockey" profiled Alex Ovechkin. Elliot Friedman led into the report with the following statement:

> *You could make a real argument that he is the most popular non-North American ever in the NHL. Why? Because Alexander Ovechkin will try anything.*

With this lead-in, the feature on Ovechkin included an excerpt from a Russian TV show called Ты! Не Поверишь (*You! Don't Believe*). In the excerpt, Ovechkin gives out a cell number for girls to call to arrange a date with him. "Girls," he begins, "I'm gonna give out my telephone number, but I'm gonna leave out two numbers… The first girl that calls me on the phone will get a date with me." And then he reads the number, with two of the numbers scrambled. It remains unclear whether anyone correctly guessed the missing two digits and got the date.

The Human Touch

During the 2007–08 season, a Buffalo Sabres' fan posted a story on the Washington Capitals' online fan board about a meeting with Alex Ovechkin. The woman who posted the story had just seen a game between Buffalo and Washington with her family—which includes a seven-year-old daughter who is a huge Ovechkin fan and had recently been diagnosed with leukemia. The woman managed to get Washington's PR department to have Ovechkin pay the young girl a visit and later posted this story:

> *When Alex and some other guy walked in the room her little jaw dropped and she just stared at him.... She told him about how she plays, or played rather, hockey and he gave her a few tips, lol. She told him about how she had a chemo treatment that morning and she wasn't feeling too well and he gave her another hug.... He even gave her a "special" nickname: Lulu, lol. I asked him why Lulu, and he said because he likes that name, lol. He's a funny guy.... I just wanted everyone to know what an AMAZING guy we have here in Washington. I've never had an experience quite like that one.*

The Crazy Eights

"Ovi's Crazy Eights" is a community-based program that was established by Ovechkin in 2006. Like the card game Crazy Eights (and like Ovechkin himself), the idea is that eights are wild. Each year, Ovechkin purchases eight tickets to every Capitals' home game and donates them to a local community group called Most Valuable Kids (MVK). In turn, MVK distributes the tickets to eight underprivileged children and/or soldiers from the Washington/Baltimore area.

MVK's goal is to provide kids with a means of coming face to face with their role models, to foster the development of self-esteem and to provide them with an appreciation of the benefits of self-discipline, perseverance and hard work.

The Russian Voice

The freedom of the Internet has opened up so many new landscapes for broadcasting and advertising that a lot of online content is downright puzzling. Because the Internet provides a forum that enables anyone to express him- or herself, there is no quality control. It is a sad reality that the cost of traditional forms of journalism can no longer compete with the free information available online.

As an example of what happens when random people report the news, here is a journalistic article that appeared on the website HockeyPolls.com after Ovechkin hit the 50-goal plateau towards the end of the 2008–09 season. The writer is describing the goal, Ovechkin's greatness and his controversial celebration that had Don Cherry up in arms. The "stick on fire" celebration was widely criticized for being yet another sample of Ovechkin's excessive showmanship.

Although the writing is almost incomprehensible, it is a fascinating example of what happens when a Russian speaker tries to emulate North American hockey slang. If one thing is clear, it is that the writer is enraptured by Ovechkin's greatness:

- *Ovechkin scored his NHL-leading 50th goal to become Washington's first three-time 50-goal scorer. That was the recording books.*

- *Every body of every ones from overly in favor of their screaming and cheering has to be at the same time. After the unforgettable goal, not every body was able to forget the favorable scorer through the loudly cheers.*

- *First, Ovechkin followed through with a plan in his mind, thought of the smart mint. Secondly, he creditably pretended to warm his hands ready for a kick over it and he let it work.*

- *I didn't know what to expect from this terrific player as he is. He every times went down a notch in my kind of books. Even though I realize still like Crosby, boy that Ovechkin too much over scary.*

Chapter Eight

Quotes, Statistics, Awards and Records

Quotes from Ovechkin on Himself

My biggest weapon isn't my shot. It's me.

━━◆━━

I want to be number one because I always want to be number one. If I play, I want to be number one. If I'm drafted, I want to be number one. Always number one.

–Stated on the eve of the 2004 NHL Entry Draft

━━◆━━

It's like a child getting his most secret dream achieved. For example, if you always dreamed about a toy Transformer robot and you finally get it. That's what I feel on the ice.

–Describing (through an interpreter) what it's like to play hockey at the NHL level

━━◆━━

It's good to be Ovi.

━━◆━━

I'm okay. Russian machine never breaks.

———◆———

I wear tinted visor not to trick other players, but so hot girls in stands don't see me looking at them.

———◆———

When I wake up now, I don't have breakfast. I try to make something, but it's no good. I just go to Starbucks and eat chocolate.

———◆———

Quotes from Ovechkin on Sidney Crosby

Sometimes I think about Crosby, and sometimes I don't think about Crosby. Right now I don't think about him because he is he and I am I.

–When asked during his rookie season whether he concerns himself with the comparisons between himself and Crosby

———◆———

Question:

Isn't Crosby your main opponent for the title of the best rookie in the NHL?

Ovechkin:

So what? He is a great player. Though, I was somewhat responsible in quieting down a wave of "Sidneymania" that [was] sweeping Canada…Every interview always

ended with the same question: Who's better—you or Crosby? I was so sick of that question that when we played Canada at the Olympics, I didn't need to look for any additional motivation. After I scored the winning goal against the Maple Leafs [the nickname of Team Canada in Russia], *they stopped asking me about Crosby. But that's the only nice memory of those Games.*

❖

What can I say about Crosby? He is a good player, but he talks too much. I play hard and if he wants to hit me, he can hit me, not talk to you guys about who plays cheap and who plays dirty. That's my game. If he doesn't like it, that's his problem.

❖

What, I can't play hard against him. What's he going to do, cry?

❖

Quotes from Ovechkin on Fame

When I see a little boy, I remember when I was little and I used to stand and wait for some guy I would go to after a game. They are fans, and they want my signature. They live in Washington, and they are fans of our team. I think if I signed 10 signatures and there were 20 more fans waiting and I didn't sign for them also, they would want to know why, and I would feel bad. If you have time, why not sign them all?

———◆———

Nothing changes. If you are a great hockey player, you must be a great man.

—When asked about whether fame changes anything

———◆———

Money is money. But a dream is a dream.

———◆———

Quotes from Ovechkin on Hockey

That's hockey. You never know what's going to happen. It's a tough sport. No tooth, a broken nose, but I'm looking good.

———◆———

For me, it doesn't matter where I play. If coach says I must play goalie, I will play goalie.

———◆———

I want to win the Stanley Cup. I want to be the best, just the best. I must work. I must learn. Help my team. Play hockey, that's all. Hockey is my life, you know. If I do not play hockey, I do not know what I do.

———◆———

I saw the rebound and when the puck came to me, I said, "Oh my god, puck; I must shoot."

———◆———

Reporter:

What is the greatest thing about playing in the NHL?

Ovechkin:

NHL.

Reporter:

The NHL?

Ovechkin nods his head and walks away.

———◆———

Quotes from Ovechkin on Russia

[In the U.S.] *you see 65 (miles per hour) and you can go 80. In Russia, you see 65 and you can go 100 or whatever you want. Just give the police some money.*

———◆———

I have kept good relationships with everyone at Dynamo. I got a little sense of nostalgia, when I walked around the training facility [that is] *so dear to me. A lot of things changed for the better. For example, the team museum expanded with new items. But the main thing is that the same people are still*

working there. I was met with lots of kind-
ness and open arms.

–After visiting the Dynamo Sports Club
during the summer of 2007

Quote from Ovechkin on America

Question:

What has America taught you?

Ovechkin:

Probably independence. When I played for
Dynamo, my mom and dad were always
with me, taking care of everything. In the
U.S., my brother Misha (now a student at
Georgetown University) and I found our-
selves one on one with the world. It turned
out that even making dinner was a project!
When we tried to make a dish for the first
time, it went straight into garbage. Thank-
fully, our American friends, seeing our
"suffering," took us under their wings.
My agent Susan would often fly in from
Toronto and live with us for weeks: cooking,
cleaning, and giving us hell for making
a mess in the house.... Another agent, Sergei
Isakov, turned out to be a decent cook—made
soups, meat and fish that made you want
to lick your fingers.

Quotes from Others on Ovechkin

This guy is becoming a kind of folk hero in hockey.

–Ted Leonsis, Washington Capitals' owner

That guy's crazy. He has tons of fun playing, looks like he's having too much fun and he works hard. It's definitely a game for him and he enjoys every moment of it. That's why he's so good at it.

–Ray Emery, Philadelphia Flyers

I've got to tell you, I love the kid. He's the only guy I've ever coached against who scored a goal and blew me a kiss. Pretty good goal, too. You can see he loves to play.

–Wayne Gretzky

The more you hit him, the more physical he gets, and the more into it he gets as well.

–Jay Harrison, Toronto Maple Leafs

More and more players are talking about this guy like they're fans of his.

–Brendan Shanahan, New Jersey Devils

He's got a tremendous will to score.

–Paul Kariya, St. Louis Blues

He's Kovalchuk when Kovalchuk started. He'll go in traffic 100 miles per hour. He doesn't care about getting hurt because he's so big. Now Kovalchuk sits back and looks for one-timers.

–Martin Brodeur, New Jersey Devils

Speed, strength, reach, shot, moves. You can't stop him. He's got options…and he plays like he's having fun. He hits people. He gets hit, and he smiles. We were playing there [in Washington] *one day and he went to hit Bouillon. Bouillon comes back at him and hits him pretty good. Cuts him.* [Ovechkin] *skates by our bench and says, 'That was a good hit!' I don't know if he knew at that point his nose was broken.*

–Guy Carbonneau, ex-coach of the Montréal Canadiens

The best tip Ovi has given me is to take it easy at the bars.

–Nicklas Backstrom, Ovechkin's young Swedish centerman

He's like the shark in Jaws, *circling in the water waiting for blood. They should play that music from the movie—da-duh, da-duh, da-duh—when he's out on a shift. He doesn't just go after loose pucks; he hunts them down.*

–John Davidson, general manager and president of hockey operations for the St. Louis Blues

He's amazing. There aren't enough words in English or Russian to describe him.

–Chris Drury, New York Rangers

He's Pavel Bure in Mark Messier's body.

–George McPhee, general manager of the Washington Capitals

Alex plays harder than Kovalchuk. Is [Ovechkin] *the most talented guy I've ever played with? Yep. That's because he uses his talent to the fullest all the time. Jagr was obviously very talented, but there were nights he didn't show up. Jags didn't have the speed and the edge this guy has.*

–Olaf Kolzig, former Capitals' goalie

Alex, it's amazing what he can do. He's a great leader on the ice. He sparks the team. He believes, so we believe.

–Shaone Morrisonn, Washington Capitals

I just kiss him on his eye, and I say, "You are a great man, a strong man."

–Veronika Dyvanskaya, former girlfriend

He can take care of himself. Hockey is a very difficult sport. It's not like chess or golf. You have to be a real man, a strong man and a very brave man to play hockey.

–Tatiana Ovechkina, Ovechkin's mother

The media attention doesn't affect him. How can I put this? He came to conquer America. With the help of the guys on his team, he will conquer the United States. And it is not a bad thing to be Russian and to be recognized on the street.

–Mikhail Ovechkin, Alexander's father
(through an interpreter)

Statistics

Russian Super League and NHL Statistics

Season	Team	League	Regular Season				
			GP	G	A	Pts	PIM
2001–02	Dynamo Moscow	RSL	21	2	2	4	4
2002–03	Dynamo Moscow	RSL	40	8	7	15	29
2003–04	Dynamo Moscow	RSL	53	13	10	23	4
2004–05	Dynamo Moscow	RSL	37	13	14	27	32
		RSL Totals	151	36	33	69	69
2005–06	Washington Capitals	NHL	81	52	54	106	52
2006–07	Washington Capitals	NHL	82	46	46	92	52
2007–08	Washington Capitals	NHL	82	65	47	112	40
2008–09	Washington Capitals	NHL	79	56	54	110	72
		NHL Totals	324	219	201	420	216

Russian Super League and NHL Statistics

Season	Team	League	Playoffs				
			GP	G	A	Pts	PIM
2001–02	Dynamo Moscow	RSL	3	0	0	0	0
2002–03	Dynamo Moscow	RSL	5	0	0	0	2
2003–04	Dynamo Moscow	RSL	3	0	0	0	2
2004–05	Dynamo Moscow	RSL	10	2	4	6	31
		RSL Totals	21	2	4	6	35
2005–06	Washington Capitals	NHL	—	—	—	—	—
2006–07	Washington Capitals	NHL	—	—	—	—	—
2007–08	Washington Capitals	NHL	7	4	5	9	0
2008–09	Washington Capitals	NHL	14	11	10	21	8
		NHL Totals	21	15	15	30	8

International Statistics

Year	Team	Event	GP	G	A	Pts	PIM
2002	Russia	U18	8	14	4	18	0
2003	Russia	WJC*	6	6	1	7	4
2003	Russia	U18	6	9	4	13	6
2004	Russia	WJC*	6	5	2	7	25
2004	Russia	WC**	6	1	1	2	0
2004	Russia	WCH**	2	1	0	1	0
2005	Russia	WJC*	6	7	4	11	4
2005	Russia	WC**	8	5	3	8	4
2006	Russia	Oly**	8	5	0	5	8
2006	Russia	WC**	7	6	3	9	6
2007	Russia	WC**	8	1	2	3	29
2008	Russia	WC**	9	6	6	12	8
**Senior Totals			48	25	15	40	55
*U20 Totals			18	18	7	25	33
U18 Totals			14	23	8	31	6

Legend	
U18	Under 18
U20	Under 20
WJC	World Junior Championship
WC	World Championship
WCH	World Cup of Hockey
Oly	Olympics
GP	Games Played
G	Goals
A	Assists
Pts	Points
PIM	Penalty Minutes

All-Star Games				
Year	Location	G	A	Pts
2007	Dallas	1	0	1
2008	Atlanta	2	0	2
2009	Montreal	1	2	3
	All-Star Totals	4	2	6

Awards

NHL

- NHL Rookie of the Month: December 2005 and January 2006

- NHL Offensive Player of the Week: weeks ending December 31, 2005; January 23, 2006

- Calder Memorial Trophy (NHL Rookie of the Year): 2006

- NHL All-Rookie Team: 2006

- NHL Offensive Player of the Month: January 2006

- NHL First All-Star Team: 2006, 2007, 2008, 2009

- Kharlamov Trophy (Best Russian Player): 2006, 2007, 2008, 2009

- NHL Number One Star of the Week: weeks ending December 30, 2007; March 9, 2008; March 23, 2008; December 28, 2008.

- NHL Number One Star of the Month: January 2008, March 2008, November 2008

- NHL All-Star Game Selections: 2007, 2008, 2009

- NHL Player of the Year, *Sporting News*: 2008, 2009

- Art Ross Trophy: 2008 (112 points)

- Lester B. Pearson Award (Most Outstanding Player): 2008, 2009

- Hart Memorial Trophy (Most Valuable Player): 2008, 2009

- Maurice "Rocket" Richard Trophy: 2008 (65 goals), 2009 (56 goals)

International Play

- 2005 World Junior Ice Hockey Championships: Best Forward

- 2006 Winter Olympics: Ice Hockey All-Tournament Team

- 2006 IIHF World Championship: Media All-Star Team

- 2008 IIHF World Championship: Media All-Star Team

Records

NHL Records

- First player to win the Art Ross Trophy, Maurice Richard Trophy, Lester B. Pearson Award and Hart Memorial Trophy in a single season

- Most points scored by a rookie left winger (2005–06): 106 points

- Most shots on goal by a rookie in a season (2005–06): 425 shots

- Most regular season points by a Russian-born NHL rookie (2005–06): 106 points

- Point streak in consecutive games to start an NHL career by a number-one overall pick (2005–06): 8 games

- Fastest overtime goal: 6 seconds, December 15, 2006, vs. Atlanta Thrashers (tied with Mats Sundin and David Legwand)

- Most goals scored by a left winger in a season (2007–08): 65 goals

- Most shots on goal by a left winger in a season (2008–09): 528 shots

Washington Capitals Records

- Most goals in a season by a rookie (2005–06): 52 goals

- Most points in a season by a rookie (2005–06): 106 points

- Point streak by a rookie to start season: 8 games

- Goal streak by a rookie: 7 games, February 10 to March 8, 2006

- Point streak by a rookie: 11 games (5 goals, 12 assists, 17 points), March 18 to April 7, 2006

- Most seasons with 50 or more goals: 3 (2005–06, 2007–08, 2008–09)

- Most goals in a season (2007–08): 65 goals

- Most shots on goal in a season: 528 (2008–09)

Notes on Sources

Introduction

sportsillustrated.cnn.com/vault/article/magazine/
MAG1105914/index.htm

Chapter One

sportsillustrated.cnn.com/vault/article/magazine/
MAG1109692/2/index.htm

www.washingtonpost.com/wp-dyn/content/article
/2006/02/04/AR2006020400979.html

www.washingtonpost.com/wp-dyn/content/article
/2006/11/21/AR2006112101807.html (five-page
article on family)

www.washingtonpost.com/wp-dyn/content/article
/2006/11/21/AR2006112101807_2.html

www.washingtontimes.com/news/2008/jun/24/
districts-other-ovechkin/?page=2

Chapter Two

en.wikipedia.org/wiki/Dynamo_Sports_Club

en.wikipedia.org/wiki/Order_of_Lenin

en.wikipedia.org/wiki/Roman_Abramovich

hotleaderceleb.blogspot.com/2008/05/who-is-
alexander-ovechkin-girlfriend.html

vault.sportsillustrated.cnn.com/vault/article/magazine
/MAG1109692/index.htm

www.izvestia.ru/weekend/article3116601/

www.russianprospects.com/public/article.php?article
_id=197

www.washingtonpost.com/wp-dyn/content/discussion
/2006/11/22/DI2006112201509.html

Chapter Three

74.125.47.132/search?q=cache:Y4W6_r1aQnYJ:law.
marquette.edu/s3/site/images/sports/Annualsports.
espn.go.com/nhl/recap?gameId=251005023

Survey.doc+ovechkin+moscow+dynamo+recruit&cd
=14&hl=en&ct=clnk&gl=ca&client=firefox-a (contract with Dynamo, Avangard, Caps)

www.businesswire.com/portal/site/google/index.
jsp?ndmViewId=news_view&newsId=200602280059
79&newsLang=en

vault.sportsillustrated.cnn.com/vault/article/magazine
/MAG1105914/index.htm

www.bukisa.com/articles/32646_alexander-ovechkin-
capitals-career

www.ovechkinfans.com/AO-SI.html (Michael Farber
SI article)

www.youtube.com/watch?v=UUQCGYPeCck

Chapter Four

forums.internationalhockey.net/showthread.
php?t=4201

Chapter Five

en.wikipedia.org/wiki/Evgeni_Malkin

en.wikipedia.org/wiki/Ilya_Kovalchuk

en.wikipedia.org/wiki/Pavel_Bure

en.wikipedia.org/wiki/Pavel_Datsyuk

en.wikipedia.org/wiki/Sergei_Gonchar

sabreslegends.blogspot.com/2009/03/alexander-
mogilny.html

sports.espn.go.com/nhl/news/story?id=3541663

www.cbssports.com/nhl/story/9740727

www.pbs.org/wgbh/pages/frontline/shows/hockey/
etc/script.html

www.post-gazette.com/pg/06274/726598-61.stm

www.tsn.ca/nhl/story/?id=278120

Chapter Six

ballhype.com/video/alexander_ovechkin_scores_an_
amazing_goal_capitals/

www.youtube.com/watch?v=KAdg2Gy09sg

www.youtube.com/watch?v=d6EJ5Iwnv9w&feature
=related

Chapter Seven

alexovetjkin.blogspot.com/2008/02/alex-ovechkins-
love-story.html

pittsburgh.bizjournals.com/pittsburgh/stories/2008/
08/11/focus4.html

sportsillustrated.cnn.com/vault/article/magazine/
MAG1109692/index.htm

vault.sportsillustrated.cnn.com/vault/article/magazine/
MAG1109692/index.htm www.ocregister.com/sports/
nhl-players-concussions-1850188-league-head

www.urbandictionary.com/define.php?term=rockstar

www.youtube.com/watch?v=5_dYU2tslnU&feature=
related

www.youtube.com/watch?v=d4C_MipzPTE

www.youtube.com/watch?v=H4xBKCJnIjI&NR=1

Chapter Eight

hfboards.com/showthread.php?t=248393

Geoffrey Lansdell

Geoffrey Lansdell is a sportswriter who grew
up in Victoria, British Columbia, and for the
past 12 years, he has lived in Montréal, Québec.
As a kid, he collected hockey cards, listened to
Vancouver Canuck broadcasts on the radio and
idolized Tony Tanti. He has written sports and pop
culture articles for the online men's magazine
AskMen.com, and in 2008, he wrote *Weird Facts
About Curling,* an anecdotal saga about the odd
world of curling. Like most rabid hockey fans,
he has cheered on the exploits of the reigning
MVP of the NHL, Alexander Ovechkin.